Monologion and Proslogion
with the Replies of Gaunilo and Anselm

CONTENTS

NOTE ON THE TRANSLATION

My aim has been to produce as literal a translation as possible while respecting contemporary English idiom. In the works translated here, especially the *Monologion* and the exchange with Gaunilo, Anselm is concerned not with elegance of style but with rigor of argumentation. I have made every effort to represent his arguments accurately and in a way that would be as readily intelligible as possible. In the *Proslogion* Anselm's writing is much less utilitarian. His style there draws liberally on Scriptural language that would have felt just a little exalted and occasionally archaic without being stilted. I have tried to represent that with a style that, I hope, conveys something of the same feeling. As for Gaunilo's reply, I have been somewhat less literal there. Gaunilo's Latin is often inelegant, and a literal translation would not have been fair to his arguments, which, while not always very well formulated, are (I believe) a good deal more cogent than interpreters have given them credit for being.

In saying that this translation is literal I do not mean to imply that I have slavishly followed the word order or the periphrastic constructions of the Latin original. Whenever rearrangement or simplification could make a passage more readily intelligible (or even just more idiomatic) without misrepresenting Anselm's argument, I have not hesitated to rearrange or simplify. To give an example of the sort of thing I mean: in one place Anselm lists the four elements as "earth, water, air, and fire." The natural word order in English is "earth, air, fire, and water," and I have translated accordingly. But there are other, more daring, departures from strict "literal" translation that are worth mentioning.

First, the passive voice in English is often either flabby or pompous; its Latin equivalent is rarely so. Translating a Latin passive as an English passive therefore often produces a needlessly limp translation of what was a perfectly innocent Latin sentence. With this fact in mind I have not scrupled to translate Latin passive-voice verbs with English active-voice verbs and to supply the necessary subject.

Similarly, a string of negative words is enough to sap the life out of any English sentence and very often to produce needless confusion. Latin, by contrast, can make freer use of its negatives without materially injuring a sentence. When necessary, then, I have resolved strings of negatives into their affirmative equivalent.

I have not gone so far in this stylistic tidying-up, however, as to standardize Anselm's terminology. I have, for example, consistently translated *'essentia'* and *'substantia'* as 'essence' and 'substance'. Anselm's usage of *'essentia'* in particular varies widely. Sometimes it means 'essence' in the sense to which the word 'essential' corresponds, but sometimes it means 'existence' and sometimes 'substance' (in the sense of "individual subsistent thing"). In some cases it is not altogether clear which meaning is intended. Rather than "clarifying" Anselm I have simply translated *'essentia'* as 'essence' and left the work of interpretation to the reader.

Similarly, I have not insisted on differentiations that were not at work in Anselm's usage. For example, Anselm uses *'creare'* and *'facere'* as synonyms. I began by trying to translate them consistently as 'create' and 'make', but this proved not only pointless but ungainly, since Anselm so frequently uses the expression *'ea quae facta sunt'*. To insist on translating that as "the things that have been made" when "created things" means *exactly* the same thing would have been to succumb to that superstitious view of literal translation according to which there should be a one-to-one mapping of English words onto Latin.

I have regularly used 'he' to refer to God, even when the antecedent is some expression that would more naturally require 'it'. There is some justification for this in the fact that Anselm himself sometimes slips and uses a masculine pronoun where a feminine or neuter pronoun is required, but the real justification is purely practical. 'It' has to serve a variety of grammatical purposes in English, and allowing 'he' a privileged place as a personal pronoun allowed me to avoid ambiguity in dozens of otherwise intractable passages. Where the antecedent is "the Word" or "the love," referring to the second and third persons of the Trinity, I begin by using 'it' but switch to 'he' when it becomes apparent that the referent is a divine person.

Finally, the reader should be aware that Anselm's use of modal expressions is quite different from ours. For example, if Anselm says, "if p, then *necesse est* q," he generally does not mean that "necessarily q" follows from p; he need not even mean that "if p, then q" is necessarily true. He is merely using *"necesse est"* to mark an inference. In English we do this with the word 'must', and so Anselm's "if p, then *necesse est* q" becomes "if p, then it must be the case that q." Unfortunately it is not always possible in this way to save Anselm from appearing to make outrageous modal claims. Readers who are alert to issues of modality should therefore be cautious about interpreting modal words as they would in contemporary texts.

The translation was made from the critical edition of F. S. Schmitt, O.S.B., *S. Anselmi Cantuariensis Achiepiscopi Opera Omnia* (Stuttgart-Bad Cannstatt: Friedrich Fromann Verlag, 1968), I: 1–139, II: 289–290. On I: 75 I have assumed that the correction of *'scire'* to *'sciri'* should apply to line 14 rather than line 13, as is indicated in the *corrigenda* (II: 289), and on I: 116, line 2, I have followed the manuscripts and read *'ibi'* rather than *'tibi'* (see the correction on II: 290); otherwise I have followed the editor.

An asterisk in the text indicates that the word so marked is explained in the Glossary. I have generally marked such terms only on their first occurrence in a chapter and in passages where their use seems especially liable to cause misunderstanding.

I first translated the *Proslogion* for use in my Introduction to Philosophy class at the University of Notre Dame. I wish to thank my students there, as well as my students at Creighton University, both at the introductory level and in upper-division courses. From them I have learned a great deal about how to make my translation of Anselm as accessible as it is possible for a medieval philosopher to be, as well as how to protect someone encountering Anselm for the first time from needless confusions. I am grateful to Douglas K. Blount, John F. Corvino, and Brian Rak for their suggestions regarding the introduction, and to Alfred J. Freddoso for his valuable help with both the introduction and the translation. And I am especially grateful to Pat Lazure, whose spirited attack on Anselm in my introductory class at Creighton started me on a series of reflections that eventually transformed my understanding of Anselm's natural theology. I have tried to incorporate as much as possible of this new understanding in the introduction to this volume, but my debt to Mr. Lazure for breathing new life into that professorial commonplace about how much we learn from our students is far greater than I can make apparent here.

INTRODUCTION

Philosophers have long been so intrigued with Anselm's cele-
brated "ontological argument"—and understandably so—that it
has been all too easy for them to ignore the rest of the *Monologion*
and *Proslogion*. But in fact it is impossible to do justice to Anselm's
natural theology without careful attention to the whole of both
works. In what follows, therefore, I have attempted to provide a
road map through the *Monologion* and the *Proslogion*, paying special
attention to the internal structure of each work and the connections
between the two. Along the way I have interspersed commentary
in which I try show how the various parts of the works fit into
Anselm's project as a whole and to answer questions that frequently occur to readers encountering Anselm for the first time.

I.

The *Monologion* begins with several arguments for the existence of
God, arguments that Anselm thinks will convince even an unbeliever. Now right at the outset we are faced with an obvious
question. Isn't the enterprise of natural theology—the attempt to
prove the existence and nature of God by reason alone, without
relying on revelation—just a kind of intellectual parlor game?
After all, Anselm was a monk, writing for his brother monks.
Obviously they were not on the edge of their seats as they worked
through the *Monologion*, in agonizing suspense to see whether
God really existed after all. They already believed in God and
would go on believing whether a successful argument for God's
existence was forthcoming or not. So at first glance Anselm's
project in the *Monologion* might seem rather fishy.

A careful look at the contents of the *Monologion* actually rein-
forces this suspicion. Anselm was passionate and engaging, we
are told, and he could write beautiful and captivating prose when
he set his mind to it. But for long stretches of the *Monologion*
Anselm shows us very little of this passion, and his only conces-
sions to rhetoric seem perfunctory and halfhearted. Instead we

find him dispassionately constructing arguments and analyzing language; and while his arguments certainly stimulate the mind, they do little to captivate the heart. To make matters worse, Anselm already knows what conclusions he must reach in the arguments he constructs and what meanings he must find in the language he analyzes. One begins to wonder whether natural theology is nothing but a philosophical crossword puzzle, a test of ingenuity with a ready-made solution.

So why bother doing natural theology at all? Or more to the point, what is *Anselm* up to when he does natural theology? The obvious answer is that he wants to know the truth. But this answer explains very little until we recognize that for Anselm the truth is not some sort of wispy ideal but an actual concrete *person*. The truth is God; to know the truth means to know God. And so the ultimate aim of natural theology is not knowledge in the sense of *information* but knowledge in the sense of *acquaintance*. Anselm intended his arguments to provide us with a way of becoming acquainted with God.

Now if the truth is a person, we can expect it to have hard edges. To understand what I mean by "hard edges," consider the analogy of getting to know a friend. I did not become acquainted with my friends through a quick flash of effortless insight; they are far too complicated for me to come to know them so easily. They do not simply conform to my expectations as if they were characters I was making up out of my own head. They are complex, subtle, nuanced, sometimes baffling, but always unmistakably themselves. Getting to know them means getting to know these hard edges, the rich and varied traits they have quite independently of whether I happen to find out about them, traits that I may discover but certainly do not create.

If it is difficult for us to get to know our friends, with whom we share a common human nature, we can certainly expect that getting to know the person who is truth will be very hard work indeed, since he enjoys an existence far superior to and unimaginably different from our own. Anselm does that work in those difficult passages of bare-bones argumentation. He is trying to come to know a personal truth of such complexity that he needs all the discipline and patience he can command in order to make progress.

One should therefore not wonder where Anselm's passion has gone when he is doing natural theology. The passion is there all along. Anselm cares passionately about loving God, and so he cares passionately about knowing God. But the God he longs to know stretches human reason to its limits. To return to my earlier metaphor: in a landscape of hard edges, it pays to watch your step. The person who carefully considers every move may appear less passionate than the one who rushes eagerly ahead, but she is more likely to reach her destination. The truly passionate person is the one who cares so deeply about reaching her destination that she is willing to ponder every difficult step along the way.

II.

The motto "faith seeking understanding" is often associated with Anselm; in fact, it was the original title of the book he later renamed *Proslogion*. As philosophers typically explain it, the idea of faith seeking understanding means that Anselm begins by believing in God, but merely believing does not satisfy him. He wants to *understand* what he believes. That is, he wants reasons to believe it, proofs that it is true. The implication is that faith strikes Anselm as a little shady, whereas understanding is quite respectable. So the believer who can replace his faith with understanding has made progress in a very desirable way.

But from what I have said so far it should be clear that this way of thinking about faith seeking understanding misrepresents what Anselm is doing. Consider again the analogy between discovering the truth and getting to know a person. Faith is like the initial attraction you might feel for someone you have just met. When you feel such an attraction, you want to get to know that person better. Understanding is like a full-fledged friendship, an intimate knowledge of the friend in all his complexities. Thus, the project of faith seeking understanding is like the activity of working to develop a friendship.

When faith seeking understanding is interpreted in this way, it is clear that Anselm is not hoping to *replace* faith with understanding. You do not work at a friendship in order to get rid of that initial attraction; indeed, if all goes well, the attraction becomes stronger as you get to know your friend better. I say "if all goes well" because of course in human friendship, you can find that the initial attraction dies when the person turns out not to be what you had hoped. But there is no such risk in faith seeking understanding, Anselm believes, because the better you come to know God the more you will see that he is worthy of all your love. So faith is the passion that sets Anselm on the arduous road to understanding; and understanding, far from replacing that passion, feeds it, focuses it, and makes it all the more powerful. It should be no surprise, therefore, that at the end of the *Monologion*, after all the arguments have been weighed and a measure of understanding has been achieved, Anselm is still talking about faith, and how we can tell living faith from dead faith.

III.

Since Anselm's aim is to acquaint us with the personal truth that is God, he recognizes that merely proving the existence of God is not of much value. We want to know not merely whether God exists but what he is like. Anselm therefore devotes chapters 5–65 (by far the largest section of the *Monologion*) to discussing the divine attributes. He first (in chapters 5–14) discusses God's relation to his creatures, taking pains to emphasize God's complete independence from his creatures and their complete dependence on him.

In chapters 15–27 Anselm explicates and argues for his understanding of God's simplicity, eternity, omnipresence, and immutability. Two features of these discussions are especially noteworthy. First, Anselm often presents arguments hypothetically. That is, he lays down a hypothesis, shows what that hypothesis implies, and then accepts or rejects the hypothesis depending on whether those implications are true or false. Often, in fact, he will use such a hypothetical investigation to show that the hypothesis is true if it is understood in one sense but false if understood in another sense. This procedure is usually clear enough when it is carried out on a small scale, but it can be confusing when (as in chapters 20 and 21) an entire chapter is one elaborate hypothetical investigation. In chapter 20 Anselm argues that if God is omnipresent and eternal, he exists in *every* place and time; then in chapter 21 he turns around and argues that if God is simple and immutable, he exists in *no* place or time. It is not until chapter 22 that he explains how both of these conclusions can be true, as long as we understand the expressions in the right way.

This point brings us to the second important feature of Anselm's discussions in chapters 15–28 (and indeed throughout the *Monologion*). As I have already pointed out, Anselm seems excessively concerned with questions about the proper use of language. For example, what exactly does 'nothing' mean when it is said that God "created all things from nothing"? What exactly does 'everywhere' mean when it is said that God "is present everywhere"? In part this is simply a concern for accurate expression that Anselm shares with most other philosophers. After all, it is not perfectly obvious at first glance what it would mean to say that God created everything "from nothing," and if Christians are going around saying this without knowing what it means, they are simply mouthing empty words. Moreover, some of the things that the expression *might* mean are very odd (as Anselm shows), and it is important to guard against misinterpretation.

Even more important is this: by analyzing certain key expressions he has inherited from Scripture and tradition, Anselm can gain much greater clarity about the nature of God himself. So, for example, the problem with misunderstanding the claim that "God created everything from nothing" is not simply that one might hold an odd view, but that one might think unworthily about God and his relation to his creatures. Systematic reflection on the language of Christian doctrine is therefore not "mere semantics"; it is always in the service of a better understanding of God. So when you are faced with a passage of linguistic analysis whose point seems obscure, ask yourself questions like these: What views of the divine nature is Anselm trying to guard against here? And why does he regard such views as misunderstandings? Is he trying to illustrate connections with other divine attributes? Is he worried about the appearance of an inconsistency with something else Christians typically say about God? If you can answer these questions, you will find that what initially seemed pointless takes on a new importance.

IV.

The understanding of God at which Anselm arrives can seem no less puzzling than the process by which he arrives there. In particular, it seems that Anselm plays fast and loose with Scripture, taking the biblical witness at face value when it happens to

agree with the results of his arguments, but more often rein-
terpreting it when it disagrees with those results. There is a great
deal of truth in this charge, but Anselm would not regard it as an
objection. In fact, I think he would point to it as another reason
why natural theology is indispensable. Consider first a very obvious case. Scripture often refers to God as a rock. We immediately recognize this as metaphorical. How? Because (Anselm
would say) reason tells us that whatever else God might be, he
simply cannot be a rock.

So if we are to sort out the metaphorical from the literal, we
must bring reason to bear on our reading of Scripture. And that
means that we must do natural theology. That is, we must use our
reason to develop an understanding of God that will enable us to
recognize when Scripture is using metaphor—not so that we can
then dismiss the metaphor as mere rhetorical ornament, but so
that we can recognize the literal truth that is being metaphorically
expressed. Anselm wrestles with this task throughout the *Monologion* and *Proslogion*. He does not simply keep silent about apparent discrepancies between his conclusions and the teachings of
Scripture in the hope that the reader will not notice them. In fact,
he goes out of his way to introduce the most recalcitrant passages
and then show what reason has to say about them.

Anselm is convinced that if our conception of God does not come
from reason, it can come only from our own imagination. This
conviction leads us to another reason that natural theology is indispensable. If the God I acknowledge and praise is a construction of
my own fancy, I am an idolater, in fact if not in intention. And at a
more fundamental level, my relationship with the ultimate truth
about the world I live in is askew. The only thing that can save me
from being out of sync with reality in this way is reason.

Anselm's confidence in reason is no longer widely shared. But it
is a consequence of his conviction that the truth is a person. But
surely we can get to know persons; we do so all the time. Of
course we never attain an exhaustive knowledge even of our
closest human friends, but through attentive observation we can
discover a great deal about them. And what observation does in
our acquaintance with human beings, reason does in our knowledge of God.

Anselm's confidence in reason also arises from his conviction
that God created human beings in his own image, and that our

ultimate happiness is to be found in knowing and loving God. Now having reason is no small part of what it means to be in the image of God. So Anselm believes that God—who is Truth himself—gave us our reason, patterned it after himself, and designed it expressly so that it could come to know him. Our reason is therefore fundamentally at home with the truth.

Notice that the two convictions that justify Anselm's confidence in reason derive from his Christian faith. So we have another sense in which Anselm's project is aptly described as faith seeking understanding: faith not only gives him the passion that impels him to investigate natural theology, it also gives him the confidence that his investigation will pay off in the end.

V.

In chapters 29–65 of the *Monologion* Anselm turns his attention to Trinitarian theology. It sometimes seems that Anselm thinks he is giving philosophical proofs of various elements of the doctrine of the Trinity, just as he gave philosophical proofs of the existence and attributes of God. But if that is what he is doing, there is something remarkably suspicious about the ease with which he manages to "prove" not merely the basic point about the threefold nature of God but even the most abstruse details of Trinitarian dogma, right down to the peculiar technical terminology ("consubstantial," "begetting," "spirating," and the like).

In fact, however, Anselm does not suppose that these arguments would be convincing to the unbeliever in the way that the proofs of the existence of God are supposed to be; and he certainly does not suppose that he, or any other philosopher, would have come up with them if God had not already revealed himself as a Trinity. Nonetheless, it must be admitted that Anselm here shows a greater confidence in the powers of reason than some other Christian philosophers. For many Christian philosophers have held that when it comes to the mysteries of the faith (like the Trinitarian nature of God), reason can at best defend them against objections and show that they involve no logical impossibilities. Anselm, however, holds that once our reason is enlightened by faith, it can come to see that these mysteries are in some sense fitting and inevitable. In other words, from the standpoint of someone who already accepts the Christian revelation, Anselm

xviii   *Introduction*

can explore the doctrine of the Trinity and show not merely that it is coherent but that it in fact makes a good deal of sense—that if only you had known how to examine the matter properly, you would have seen that something like the doctrine of the Trinity had to be true.

In the closing chapters of the *Monologion* Anselm turns his attention to the rational soul, which among all creatures is the closest image of God and therefore the vehicle through which we can best come to know God. He argues that the soul was created precisely in order that it might come to know and love God, and on that basis he constructs an argument for the immortality of the soul. Anselm concludes by considering the three theological virtues—love (chapters 68–71), hope (chapter 75), and faith (chapters 76–78)—and by offering some concluding remarks about God.

VI.

When Anselm looked back over the *Monologion* he was struck by how complicated a chain of argument it involved. So he began to look for an easier way to reach the conclusions he had argued for in the *Monologion*: a single argument that would prove everything he wanted to prove, without any need for additional supporting arguments for every different conclusion. Anselm's search for this master argument became something of an obsession with him; in fact, he tells us that he began to see it as a temptation and tried (unsuccessfully, as it turned out) to stop thinking about it.

The master argument finally came to him. It is the argument that has come to be known as the "ontological argument" and is laid out in chapter two of the *Proslogion*. The basic idea is almost perversely simple. God is, by definition, that than which nothing greater can be thought. But simply from that definition we can conclude that God does indeed exist. How so? Because, Anselm says, it is greater to exist in reality than to exist merely in the mind. Therefore, if we say that God exists only in the mind but not in reality, we must say that we can think of something greater than God. But God is that than which nothing greater can be thought, and obviously we cannot think of something greater than that than which nothing greater can be thought. So, since the assumption that God does not exist in reality leads to a contradiction, we can conclude that God does in fact exist in reality.[1]

Once the ontological argument is in place, Anselm has no difficulty in using it to prove the divine attributes as well. He announces his general strategy in chapter 5: God is whatever it is better to be than not to be. It is better to be just than not just, eternal than not eternal, omnipotent than not omnipotent, and so on. To prove that all of these attributes do indeed belong to God, Anselm simply uses the ontological argument over and over. For example: God is that than which nothing greater can be thought. It is greater to be omnipotent than not omnipotent. So suppose that God is not omnipotent. Then we could think of something greater than God. But obviously we *cannot* think of anything greater than God, since he is that than which nothing greater can be thought. Therefore, God is omnipotent.

One can easily go back and substitute other divine attributes for omnipotence and see that Anselm's master argument—if it works at all—really does generate a whole host of conclusions without any need for other arguments.[2] It produces so many conclusions, in fact, that Anselm is faced with a serious problem. For some of the divine attributes seem to conflict with others. To take one example, omnipotence seems to mean that God can do everything. But God is also supposed to be just, which seems to mean (among other things) that he cannot lie or break a promise. So which is it? Is God omnipotent, and therefore able to lie and break

1. There is a similar argument in chapter 3. The exact relationship between the two arguments—or the two versions of the same argument—is a matter of much philosophical debate. It is clear, however, that the chapter 3 argument has a stronger conclusion. In chapter 2 Anselm concludes simply that God exists, but in chapter 3 he concludes that God cannot be thought not to exist (or, in more modern terminology that is only roughly equivalent, that God exists *necessarily*). Some philosophers have argued that the chapter 3 argument is not vulnerable to the objections often brought against the chapter 2 argument.

2. But precisely because Anselm moves so quickly in establishing the divine attributes, his arguments raise many questions that are left unanswered. Fortunately the more extended arguments in the *Monologion* usually provide the necessary explanations. The Index will enable the reader to find the passages in the *Monologion* that supplement the arguments in the *Proslogion*.

promises, or is he just, and therefore not able to do everything after all?

Anselm carefully investigates these and other apparent contradictions throughout the rest of the *Proslogion*. In the case of justice and omnipotence, for example, he argues that God's omnipotence means that he has all power. But lying and promise-breaking are not evidence of power at all; they are evidence of weakness, and if God is all-powerful, he has no weakness. Therefore, God's omnipotence is not merely *consistent with* his inability to lie and break promises; it actually *entails* that inability.

VII.

Most people, on reading or hearing about the ontological argument for the first time, suspect that somehow, somewhere, Anselm has slipped something past them. The first and in many ways the keenest attempt to show how the argument goes wrong was written by a monk named Gaunilo, who is known to us solely because of his little "Reply on Behalf of the Fool." Anselm had argued in the *Proslogion* that even the fool (of whom the Psalmist wrote, "The fool has said in his heart, 'There is no God' ") would have to admit that God exists, once he thought seriously enough about the concept of that than which nothing greater can be thought. Gaunilo, arguing on the fool's behalf, insists that the fool would not have to admit any such thing. Gaunilo's "Reply on Behalf of the Fool" is included in this volume along with Anselm's emphatic reply to Gaunilo's criticisms.

SUGGESTIONS FOR FURTHER READING

There are few treatments of Anselm's thought as a whole. *A Companion to the Study of St. Anselm*, by Jasper Hopkins (Minneapolis: University of Minnesota Press, 1972), is a useful handbook designed with students in mind. More scholarly but by no means inaccessible is G. R. Evans's excellent study *Anselm and Talking about God* (Oxford: Clarendon Press, 1978). Both Hopkins and Evans emphasize the systematic character of Anselm's thought; Evans does so very fruitfully by emphasizing Anselm's analysis of the language we use to talk about God. Readers who wish to know more of Anselm's life can consult R. W. Southern's *Saint Anselm: A Portrait in Landscape* (Cambridge: Cambridge University Press, 1990).

Rather than discussing Anselm's thought as a whole, philosophers have concentrated on analysis and criticism of the so-called ontological argument found in chapters 2 and 3 of the *Proslogion*. The literature on the ontological argument is vast (not a year goes by without the appearance of a few more scholarly articles on the subject), and some of it is highly technical. The best introduction to the debate is *The Ontological Argument*, edited by Alvin Plantinga, with an introduction by Richard Taylor (Garden City, N.Y.: Anchor Books, 1965). This collection includes selections from the most important critics and defenders of the ontological argument from the Middle Ages through the twentieth century.

MONOLOGION

Prologue

Some of the brethren have often eagerly entreated me to write down some of the things I have told them in our frequent discussions about how one ought to meditate on the divine essence, and about certain other things related to such a meditation, as a sort of pattern for meditating on these things. Having more regard to their own wishes than to the ease of the task or my ability to perform it, they prescribed the following form for me in writing this meditation: absolutely nothing in it would be established by the authority of Scripture; rather, whatever the conclusion of each individual investigation might assert, the necessity of reason would concisely prove, and the clarity of truth would manifestly show, that it is the case, by means of a plain style, unsophisticated arguments, and straightforward disputation. They also insisted that I not disdain to answer even the simple and almost foolish objections that would occur to me.

Now for a long time I was reluctant to attempt this, and comparing myself to the task at hand, I tried many arguments to excuse myself. For the more they wanted what they had asked of me to be easy for them to use, the more difficult they made it for me actually to accomplish it. Finally, however, I was overcome by the modest persistence of their entreaties as well as the true worth of their eagerness, which was not to be slighted. Unwilling to do so because of the difficulty of the task and the weakness of my own talent, I set out to do as they had entreated me; but gladly, because of their charity, I accomplished it according to their directions, as far as I was able.

I was induced to do so in the hope that whatever I did would be known only to those who had required it, and that they would soon afterwards despise it as worthless and throw it away with contempt. For I know that I could not so much satisfy those who had entreated me as put an end to the entreaties that were hounding me. But somehow—I am not sure how—things did not turn out as I had hoped. Not only the brethren but also many others took the trouble to commend this writing to long remembrance, each copying it out in full for himself.

After frequently reconsidering it, I could not find that I had said anything in it that was inconsistent with the writings of the Catholic fathers, and especially with those of blessed Augustine.

3

Therefore, if it should seem to anyone that I put forth anything in this work that either is too novel or diverges from the truth, I ask that he not immediately condemn me as someone who either introduces novelties or asserts falsehoods. Rather, let him first look carefully at the books of the aforesaid teacher Augustine on the Trinity and then judge my work according to them. For in saying that the supreme Trinity can be said to be three substances, I have followed the Greeks, who confess three substances in one person by the same faith by which we confess three persons in one substance. For they signify by 'substance' in God what we signify by 'person'.[1]

Now whatever I said there is put forth in the role of someone who, by thought alone, disputes and investigates within himself things that he had not previously realized, just as I knew that they whose request I was aiming to fulfill wanted me to do.

But I entreat and eagerly beseech anyone who wishes to copy this work that he take care to put this preface at the beginning of the book before the chapter titles. For I think it is very helpful for understanding the things he will read there if someone first knows with what intention and in what way they are discussed. I also think that anyone who first sees this preface will not be quick to judge if he finds something asserted contrary to his own opinion.

---

1. See the glossary entry for substance* (3).

Chapters

Chapter 1
That there is something that is best and greatest and supreme among all existing things

If anyone does not know, either because he has not heard or because he does not believe, that there is one nature,* supreme among all existing things, who alone is self-sufficient in his eternal happiness, who through his omnipotent goodness grants and brings it about that all other things exist or have any sort of well-being, and a great many other things that we must believe about God or his creation, I think he could at least convince himself of most of these things by reason alone, if he is even moderately intelligent.

There are many ways in which he could do this, but I shall set forth the one that I think would be easiest for him. After all, everyone desires only those things that he thinks good. It is therefore easy for him to turn the eye of his mind sometimes toward investigating the source of the goodness of those things that he desires to enjoy only because he judges that they are good. Then, with reason leading and him following, he will rationally advance toward those things of which he is irrationally ignorant. But if in this I say anything that a greater authority does not teach, I wish to be understood in this way: even if I present a conclusion as necessary on the basis of arguments that seem compelling to me, I mean only that it can *seem* necessary for the time being, not that it is therefore in fact altogether necessary.

So, then, someone might easily speak silently within himself in this way: Since there are countless goods, whose great diversity we both experience through our bodily senses and discern through the reasoning of our mind, are we to believe that there is some one thing through which all goods whatsoever are good? Or are different goods good through different things? Indeed, to all who are willing to pay attention it is clear and quite certain that all things whatsoever that are said to be more or less or equally a certain way as compared to each other are said to be so through something that is not understood as different but rather as the same in diverse things, whether it is detected equally or unequally in them. For whatever just things are said to be equally or more or less just by comparison with other just things, they must be understood to be just through justice, which is not different in diverse things. Therefore, since it is certain that all goods, if they are compared to each other, are either equally or unequally good, it must be that they are all good through something that is understood to be the same in diverse good things, even though it seems that sometimes different goods are said to be good through different things.

For it seems that a horse is called good through one thing because it is strong and through another because it is fast. After all, though it seems that the horse is called good through its strength and good through its speed, it does not seem that strength is the same thing as speed. Yet, if a horse is good because it is strong or fast, how is it that a strong and fast robber is bad? So instead, just as a strong and fast robber is bad because he is harmful, so too a strong and fast horse is good because it is useful. And indeed nothing is ordinarily considered good except either because of some usefulness, as health and things that contribute to health are called good, or because of some intrinsic value, as beauty and things that contribute to beauty are regarded as good.

But since the argument we have already considered cannot be refuted in any way, it must also be the case that all useful or intrinsically valuable things, if they are genuinely good, are good through the very same thing—whatever that is—through which all goods must exist. Now who would doubt that this thing, through which all goods exist, is itself a great good? Therefore, he is good through himself, since every good exists through him. It follows, therefore, that all other things are good through something other than what they themselves are, and he alone is good through himself. Now no good that exists through another[2] is equal to or greater than that good who is good through himself. And so only he who alone is good through himself is supremely good. For something is supreme if it surpasses others in such a

---

2. The expression "through another" is frequent throughout the *Monologion*. Wherever it appears, it should be regarded as a shorthand form of "through something other than itself." Thus, when Anselm says that something "is good (or exists) through another," he means that the source of its goodness (or existence) is something other than itself. The contrast, sometimes merely implied but often expressed, is with God, who is whatever he is, not through another, but through himself.

way that it has neither peer nor superior. Now that which is supremely good is also supremely great. There is, therefore, some one thing that is supremely good and supremely great—in other words, supreme along all existing things.

Chapter 2
On the same thing

Now just as it has been found that there is something supremely good, since all good things are good through some one thing that is good through itself, in the same way it is inferred with necessity that there is something supremely great, since whatever great things exist are great through some one thing that is great through itself. Now I do not mean great in size, as a given body* is great; rather, [I mean great in the sense] that the greater something is, the better or worthier it is, as wisdom is great. And since only what is supremely good can be supremely great, there must be something greatest and best, that is, supreme among all existing things.

Chapter 3
That there is a certain nature through whom all existing things exist, and who exists through himself and is supreme among all existing things

Furthermore, not only are all good things good through the same thing, and all great things great through the same thing, but it seems that all existing things exist through some one thing. For every existing thing exists either through something or through nothing. But nothing exists through nothing. For it is not so much as conceivable that any existing thing does not exist through something. So whatever exists, exists through something. Since this is so, either there is one thing, or there are several* things, through which all existing things exist.

Now if there are several, either they are traced back to some one thing through which they [all] exist, or each of them exists through itself, or they exist through each other. But if they exist through one thing, it is no longer true that all things exist through several things; rather, all things exist through that one thing through which the several things exist.

If, however, each of them exists through itself, there is surely some one power or nature of self-existing that they have in order to exist through themselves. And there is no doubt that they exist through this one thing through which they have self-existence. Therefore, all things exist more truly through that one thing than through the several things that cannot exist without that one thing.

Now no reasoning allows for several things to exist through each other, since it is irrational to think that something exists through that to which it gives existence. For not even relatives* exist through each other in this way. For when a master and a slave stand in relation to each other, the men who stand in relation do not in any way exist through each other, and the relations by which they are related do not in any way exist through each other, since they exist through their subjects.

And so, since truth altogether rules out the possibility that there are several things through which all things exist, there must be one thing through which all existing things exist. Therefore, since all existing things exist through that one thing, undoubtedly that one thing exists through himself. So all other existing things exist through another; he alone exists through himself. Now whatever exists through another is less than the one through whom all other things exist and who alone exists through himself. Therefore, he who exists through himself exists most greatly of all things. So there is some one thing that alone exists most greatly and supremely of all things. Now he who exists most greatly of all things, and through whom exists whatever is good or great and whatever is anything at all, must be supremely good, supremely great, and supreme among all existing things. Therefore, there is something (whether he is called an essence or a substance or a nature[3]) that is best and greatest and supreme among all existing things.

Chapter 4
On the same thing

Moreover, if someone considers the natures of things, he cannot help realizing that they are not all of equal dignity; rather, some of them are on different and unequal levels. For anyone who doubts

---

3. Anselm is using these three words as synonyms. For a definition, see the glossary entry for essence* (1).

that a horse is by its very nature better than wood, and that a human being is more excellent than a horse, should not even be called a human being. Therefore, since it is undeniable that some natures are better than others, reason makes it no less obvious that one of them is so pre-eminent that he has no superior. For if this difference of levels is infinite – so that there is no level so high that an even higher level cannot be found – reason is brought to the conclusion that there is no limit to the multitude of these natures. But everyone thinks this is absurd – except for someone who is quite absurd himself. Therefore, there must be some nature* that is so superior to any other thing or things that there is nothing to which he is inferior.

Now either the nature that is like this is the only one, or there are several* like him and equal to him. Suppose they are several and equals. They cannot be equals through different things, but rather through the same thing. Now that one thing through which they are equally so great is either the very thing that they are – i.e., their essence* – or something other than what they are. Now if it is nothing other than their essence, then just as their essences are not several but one, so also the natures are not several but one. For I am here understanding nature to be the same as essence. On the other hand, if that through which those several natures are so great is other than that which they themselves are, they are certainly less than that through which they are great. For whatever is great through another is less than that through which it is great. Therefore, they are not so great that there is nothing else greater than they are. So if it is not possible either through that which they are or through something else for there to be several natures than which nothing is more excellent, there can in no way be several such natures. So the only remaining possibility is that there is one and only one nature that is so superior to the others that he is inferior to none.

Now whatever is like this is the greatest and best of all existing things. So a certain nature exists that is supreme among all existing things. But this cannot be the case unless he is through himself what he is and all existing things are through him what they are. For reason showed a little earlier that he who exists through himself, and through whom all other things exist, is supreme among all existing things. Therefore, either (conversely) he who is supreme exists through himself and all other things exist through him, or there will be several supreme beings. But it is evident that there are not several supreme beings. Therefore, there is a certain nature or substance or essence who through himself is good and great and through himself is what he is; through whom exists whatever truly is good or great or anything at all; and who is the supreme good, the supreme great thing, the supreme being or subsistent,* that is, supreme among all existing things.

Chapter 5
That, just as he exists through himself and other things exist through him, so he exists from himself and other things exist from him

And so, since what has been discovered is satisfactory, it is helpful to investigate whether this very nature, and all things that are anything, exist *from* him just as they exist *through* him. Now clearly it can be said that whatever exists *from* something also exists *through* that thing, and whatever exists *through* something also exists *from* that thing. For example, whatever exists from some matter and through a craftsman can also be said to exist through the matter and from the craftsman, since it has its existence through both and from both—that is, by both—although it does not exist through the matter and from the matter in the same way that it exists through the craftsman and from the craftsman. It follows, therefore, that just as all existing things are what they are through the supreme nature, and so he exists through himself, whereas other things exist through another, in the same way all existing things exist from that same supreme nature, and so he exists from himself, whereas other things exist from another.

Chapter 6
That he does not exist through the help of some other cause that brought him into existence, and yet neither does he exist through nothing or from nothing; and in what sense he can be understood to exist through himself and from himself

Therefore, since the expressions "to exist through something" and "to exist from something" do not always have the same meaning, we must more carefully investigate in what sense all existing things exist through or from the supreme nature. And since he who exists through himself and that which exists through another do not fit the same definition of existing, we shall first look separately at that supreme nature who exists through himself and then at those things that exist through another.

So, since it has been established that he is through himself whatever he is, and all other things are through him what they are, in what sense does he exist through himself? For whatever is said to exist through something seems to exist either through an efficient* cause or through some matter or through some other aid (for example, through a tool). Now whatever exists in any of these three ways exists through another and is both posterior* to and in some way less than that through which it has its existence. But the supreme nature in no way exists through another; nor is he posterior to or less than himself or any other thing. Therefore, the supreme nature could not come about either by his own agency or by that of some other thing, nor was he or anything else the matter from which he came about, nor did he or some other thing in any way help him to be what he was not already.

What then? Something that does not exist by the agency of something or from some matter, or come into existence by means of any aids, appears either to be nothing or, if it is something, to exist through nothing and from nothing. Now although on the basis of what has already been established by the light of reason about the supreme substance I think that these things can in no way apply to him, nonetheless, I shall not neglect to put together a proof of this. For since this meditation of mine has suddenly brought me to this important and interesting point, I do not wish to pass over any objection, however simple and almost foolish, that occurs to me in the course of my disputation. Thus, by leaving nothing doubtful in what went before, I can proceed with greater certainty to what follows; and further, if I should want to persuade anyone of what I have been thinking, even someone who is slow to understand can easily agree with what he has heard once every obstacle, however small, has been removed.

And so the claim that this nature,* apart from whom no nature at all exists, is nothing is as false as it would be absurd to say that whatever exists is nothing. Now he does not exist *through* nothing, since there is no intelligible sense in which what is something exists through nothing. But if in some sense he exists *from* nothing, he exists from nothing either through himself or through another or through nothing.

Now it has been established that in no way does something exist through nothing. Therefore, if he exists from nothing in any sense, he exists from nothing either through himself or through another. Now nothing can exist from nothing through itself, since if something exists from nothing through something, that through which it exists must exist beforehand. So, since this essence* does not exist before himself, he does not in any way exist from nothing through himself.

On the other hand, if it is said that he came to exist from nothing through some other nature, then he is not supreme among all things, but inferior to at least one; moreover, he is what he is, not through himself, but through another. Likewise, if he exists from nothing through something, that through which he exists was a great good, since it was the cause of so great a good. But no good thing can be understood [as existing] before that good without whom nothing is good. Now it is quite clear that this good, without whom no good thing exists, is the supreme nature that is under discussion. Therefore, it is not even conceivable that something preceded him through which he came to exist from nothing.

Finally, if this very nature is something either through nothing or from nothing, then undoubtedly either he is not through himself and from himself whatever he is, or he is himself said to be nothing. And there is no need to explain how false either of these alternatives is. Therefore, although the supreme substance does not exist through some efficient cause or from some matter, and although he was not helped by any causes in order that he might be brought into being, nonetheless, he does not in any sense exist through nothing or from nothing, since he is through himself and from himself whatever he is.

In what sense, then, are we to understand that he exists through himself and from himself, if he neither made himself, nor provided matter for himself, nor in any way helped himself to be what he was not already? It seems that perhaps this can be understood only in the same sense in which it is said that light shines, or is shining, through itself and from itself. For 'light' and 'to shine' and 'shining' are related to each other in just the same way as 'essence' and 'to be' and 'being', i.e., existing or subsisting.* Therefore, 'supreme essence' and 'supremely to be' and 'supremely being', i.e., supremely existing or supremely subsisting, are related to each other not unlike 'light' and 'to shine' and 'shining'.[4]

Chapter 7
In what way all other things exist through him and from him

It now remains for us to discuss the sense in which all those things that exist through another exist through the supreme substance: whether because he made them all, or because he was the matter of them all. For there is no need to ask whether they all exist through him merely because he in some way helped all things to exist, whereas some other thing made them or some other matter existed, since it is inconsistent with what became evident above if all existing things exist through him only in some secondary way and not principally.

And so I think I should first ask whether all things that exist through another exist from some matter. Now I have no doubt that the whole mass of this world with its parts, as we see it formed, consists of earth, air, fire, and water. These four elements can in some way be understood apart from the forms that we observe in formed things, in such a way that the unformed or even confused nature of the elements is seen to be the matter of all the bodies* that are made distinct by their own forms.[5] As I say, I have no doubt about that. But I ask where this thing of which I have spoken, the matter of the mass of the world, *comes from*. For if it in turn comes from some other matter, then that is more truly the matter of the physical universe.

4. The Latin words for 'light', 'to shine', and 'shining' ('*lux*', '*lucere*', and '*lucens*') are a noun, an infinitive, and a participle from the same stem. The same relation holds among the Latin words for 'essence', 'to be', and 'being' ('*essentia*', '*esse*', and '*ens*').

5. In other words, what makes one body different from another is the particular form or configuration that the elements have in that body. But you can conceive of the elements by themselves, in isolation from this or that particular configuration. When you do, you realize that the elements in this unformed state are the building blocks of all bodies.

If, then, the totality of things, whether visible or invisible, exists from some matter, it cannot exist—more than that, it cannot even be *said* to exist—from any matter other than the supreme nature, or from itself, or from some third essence that is neither. But of course nothing can even be thought to exist other than he who is supreme among all things, who exists through himself, and the totality of those things that do not exist through themselves but through that same supreme being. Therefore, that which is in no way something is not the matter of anything. But the totality of things, which does not exist through itself, cannot exist from its own nature. For if it did, it would in some way exist through itself, and through something other than the one through whom all things exist, and he would not be the only thing through which all things exist—all of which is false. Moreover, everything that exists from matter exists from another thing and is posterior* to that thing. And since nothing is other than itself or posterior to itself, it follows that nothing exists from itself materially.

But if something less than the supreme nature can exist from the matter of the supreme nature, the supreme good can be changed and corrupted—which it is impious to say. Therefore, since everything that is other than the supreme good is less than he is, it is impossible for anything else to be from him in this way. Furthermore, anything through which the supreme good is changed or corrupted is, without a doubt, in no way good. Now if any lesser nature exists from the matter of the supreme good, the supreme good is changed or corrupted through himself, since nothing exists from any source other than the supreme essence. Therefore, the supreme essence, who is himself the supreme good, is in no way good—which is a contradiction. So no lesser nature exists materially from the supreme nature. Since, therefore, it has been established that the essence of those things that exist through another does not exist from the supreme essence as its matter, nor from itself, nor from some other thing, it is evident that it exists from no matter.

Therefore, since all existing things exist through the supreme essence, and nothing can exist through him unless he either makes it or is the matter for it, it follows necessarily that nothing but him exists unless he makes it. And since nothing exists or has existed except him and the things made by him, he could not make anything at all through any instrument or assistance other than himself. Now whatever he made, he certainly made it either from something as its matter or from nothing. Therefore, since it is perfectly obvious that the essence of all things that exist, other than the supreme essence, was made by that same supreme essence, and that it does not exist from any matter, there is undoubtedly nothing more evident than this: the supreme essence alone, through himself, produced so great a mass of things—so numerous a multitude, so beautifully formed, so orderly in its variety, so fitting in its diversity—from nothing.

Chapter 8
In what sense it is to be understood
that he made everything from nothing

But something occurs to me about this 'nothing'. Whatever a thing is made from is a cause of the thing that is made from it, and, necessarily, every cause contributes some help towards the existence of the effect. This fact is so obvious to everyone from experience that no one can be talked out of it in debate, and hardly anyone can be tricked out of it through deception. Therefore, if something was made from nothing, then nothing itself was a cause of the thing that was made from nothing. But how could that which had no existence help bring something into existence? And if, on the contrary, nothing did not help bring anything into existence, who could be persuaded—and in what way—that something is brought about from nothing?

Furthermore, 'nothing' either signifies something or does not signify anything. Now if nothing is something, whatever was made from nothing was made from something. On the other hand, if nothing is not anything, then, since it is inconceivable that something is made from what does not exist at all, nothing is made from nothing—as the saying goes, "Nothing comes from nothing." From this it seems to follow that whatever exists was made from something, since it was made either from something or from nothing. Therefore, whether nothing is something or is not something, it seems to follow that whatever was made was made from something. But if this is admitted to be true, it contradicts everything that was settled above. Hence, since what was nothing will be something, what was in the greatest degree something will be nothing. After all, having found that there is a substance existing most greatly of all things, I proceeded by argument to the claim that all things were made by him in such a way that there was nothing from which they were made. Therefore, if that from which they are made – which I had thought was nothing – is in fact something, then whatever I thought I had discovered about the supreme being is nothing.

So then how is this 'nothing' to be understood? For I have already undertaken not to neglect any possible objection, foolish though it may be, in this meditation. And so it seems to me that if a substance is said to have been made from nothing, there are three ways of explaining this that would suffice to remove this present obstacle. One way is that we mean that what is said to have been made from nothing has not in fact been made at all. It is like a case in which someone asks what a silent person is talking about. "About nothing," is the answer – that is, he is not talking at all. In this sense, if someone were to ask about the supreme essence himself, or about something that did not and does not exist at all, "What was it made from?" one could correctly answer, "From nothing" – that is, it was not made at all. This sense cannot be properly applied to anything that actually has been made.

There is another meaning that can indeed be expressed but cannot be true: if something is said to have been made from nothing in the sense that it was made from nothing itself, that is, from what does not at all exist – as if nothing itself were some existing thing from which something could be made. Now since this is always false, some absurd impossibility will follow whenever it is assumed.

The third sense in which something is said to have been made from nothing is when we understand that it has indeed been made, but there was not anything from which it was made. It seems we use a similar meaning when we say that someone who is upset for no reason is upset about nothing. So if we understand our earlier conclusion in this sense, that all existing things other than the supreme essence were made by him from nothing – i.e., not from anything – then just as this conclusion follows logically from our previous conclusions, so nothing illogical will follow from it later on.

Nonetheless, it would also be logical and free from any absurdity to say that the things that were made by the creating substance were made *from* nothing in the sense in which we often say that someone has come *from* poverty to wealth or *from* sickness to health—that is, he who once was poor is now rich, which he was not before, and he who once was sick is now healthy, which he was not before. So if it is said that the creating essence made all things from nothing, or that all things were made by him from nothing, these statements can quite sensibly be understood in this sense—that is, the things that once were nothing are now something. And the expression "he made them" or "they were made" is understood to mean that when he made them, he made something, and that when they were made, they were indeed made to be something. For in the same way, when we see someone whom some man has raised from a very lowly state to great riches or honors, we say, "Look! That man made him from nothing" or "He was made from nothing by that man"—that is, he who once was regarded as nothing is now thought to be truly something, because that man has made him so.

Chapter 9
That with respect to the reason of their maker, the things that were made from nothing were not nothing before they were made

But I seem to see something that forces me to distinguish carefully the sense in which the things that were made can be said to have been nothing before they were made. After all, there is no way anyone could make something rationally unless something like a pattern (or, to put it more suitably, a form or likeness or rule) of the thing to be made already existed in the reason of the maker. And so it is clear that what they were going to be, and what sorts of things, and how they were going to be, was in the reason of the supreme nature before all things were made.

Therefore, it is clear that the things that were made were nothing before they were made, in the sense that they were not what they now are and there was not anything from which they were made. Nonetheless, they were not nothing with respect to the reason of their maker, through which and in accordance with which they were made.

Chapter 10
That this reason is an utterance of things, as a craftsman says within himself what he is going to make

Now what is that form of things that existed in his reason before the things to be created, other than an utterance of those things in his reason, just as, when a craftsman is going to make some work of his art, he first says it within himself by a conception of his mind? Now by an "utterance" of the mind or reason, I do not mean what happens when one thinks of the words that signify those things, but what happens when the things themselves (no matter whether they are yet to exist or already exist) are examined within the mind by the gaze of thought.

For we know from frequent experience that we can say one and the same thing in three ways. For we say a thing either by making perceptible use of perceptible signs, i.e., signs that can be perceived by the bodily senses; or by thinking imperceptibly within ourselves the very same signs that are perceptible when they are outside ourselves; or by not using these signs at all, whether perceptibly or imperceptibly, but rather by saying the things themselves inwardly in our mind by either a corporeal image or an understanding of reason that corresponds to the diversity of the things themselves. For example, in one way I say a man when I signify him by the word 'man', in another way when I think that same word silently, and in yet another way when my mind sees the man himself either through an image of a body (as when it imagines his sensible appearance) or through reason (as when it thinks his universal essence, which is rational, mortal animal).

Each of these three kinds of utterance corresponds to its own kind of word. But the words of the kind of utterance that I put third and last, when they are about things that are not unknown, are natural; they are the same among all peoples. Now all other words were invented on account of these natural words. Therefore, where there are natural words, no other word is necessary to know a thing; and where natural words are impossible, no other word will serve to make a thing known. And it makes good sense to say that words are truer the more similar they are to, and the more distinctly they signify, the things of which they are words. Now except for those things that we use as their own names in order to signify themselves (like certain sounds: for example, the vowel 'a')—except for those, I say, no other word seems as similar to the thing of which it is a word, or expresses it in the same way, as the likeness that is expressed in the gaze of the mind of someone who is thinking the thing itself.[6] And so that should by right be called the most proper and principal word for the thing.

So no utterance of anything whatsoever comes as close to the thing as that which consists of words of this sort. Furthermore, no other word in anyone's reason can be as similar to the thing, whether it is yet to exist or already exists. It therefore quite rightly seems that such an utterance of things not only existed in the supreme substance before the things existed, in order that through it they might be made, but also exists in him now that they have been made, in order that through it they might be known.

Chapter 11
That nonetheless there is much dissimilarity in this comparison

So it has been established that the supreme substance first said (as it were) all of creation in himself and then created it in accordance with and through that innermost utterance of his, in the way that a craftsman first conceives in his mind what he afterwards makes into a completed work in accordance with the conception of his mind. Nonetheless, I see much dissimilarity in this comparison. After all, the supreme substance collected nothing at all from any other source from which he would either assemble within himself

6. Anselm's point here is that natural words resemble the things of which they are words, whereas conventional words do not. For example, the natural word (that is, the concept) of a lion actually resembles the lion, since it is simply the mind's conception of the lion itself. The word 'lion', by contrast, does not resemble the lion much at all. It is only by convention that the word 'lion' calls up an image of a lion rather than of some other thing. There is one sort of case, however, in which conventional words do resemble the things of which they are words, and that is when we use a thing as its own name. To take Anselm's example, we use the letter 'a' as its own name. Obviously, the letter 'a' is like the letter 'a', and so the word is like the thing. But this is a limited and fairly uninteresting class of exceptions to the general rule that it is natural words that most closely resemble and most distinctly express the things of which they are words.

the form of the things he was going to make or bring it about that the things themselves exist. The craftsman, by contrast, cannot even imagine a physical object and thus conceive it in his mind unless he has somehow already come to know the object, either as a whole all at once or part by part through various things; nor can he complete the work that he has conceived in his mind if he lacks either the material or something without which the planned work cannot be made. For although a man could invent an animal the likes of which never existed, either by thinking it or by painting it, he could do this only by putting together parts stored in his memory from things he knew at another time.

Therefore, the creating substance's inward utterance of the work he is going to make differs from that of the craftsman in this respect: the Creator's utterance was not collected from or assisted by some other source; rather, as the first and sole cause it was sufficient for its Artisan to bring his work to completion. By contrast, the craftsman's utterance is neither the first nor the sole cause, and it is not sufficient for him even to get his work started. So the things that are created through the Creator's utterance are nothing at all but what they are through his utterance, whereas the things that are made through the craftsman's utterance would not be anything at all unless they were something other than what they are through his utterance.

Chapter 12
That the utterance of the supreme essence is the supreme essence

Now since by the teaching of reason it is equally certain that, whatever the supreme substance made, he did not make it through anything other than himself, and that whatever he made, he made it through his innermost utterance (whether by saying individual things by means of individual words or instead by saying all things at once by means of one word[7]), what could be seen to be any more necessary than this: the utterance of the supreme essence is nothing other than the supreme essence? And so I do not think we should carelessly neglect to consider this utterance. But

---

7. In chapter 30 Anselm resolves this question, maintaining that this utterance consists of one word, not of many words.

before we can discuss it carefully, I think we must earnestly
investigate certain properties of the supreme substance.[8]

Chapter 13
That, just as all things were made through the supreme essence, so also they remain in existence through him

Therefore, it has been established that whatever is not the same as
the supreme nature was made through him. Now only an irrational
mind could doubt that all created things remain and continue in
existence, as long as they do exist, because they are sustained by the
very same being who made them from nothing, so that they exist in
the first place. For by an exactly similar argument to the one that
shows that all existing things exist through some one thing, and so
he alone exists through himself and all other things exist through
another—by a similar argument, I say, it can be proved that everything that remains in existence does so through some one thing,
and so he alone remains in existence through himself and all other
things remain in existence through another. Now since it can only
be the case that created things remain in existence through another,
and he who created them remains in existence through himself, it
must be the case that, just as nothing was made except through the
presence of the creating essence, so nothing remains in existence
except through his conserving presence.

Chapter 14
That he exists in all things and through all things, and all things exist from him and through him and in him

If this is the case—or rather, since this is necessarily the case—it
follows that where he does not exist, nothing exists. Therefore, he
exists everywhere, both through all things and in all things. Now
no created thing can in any way pass beyond the immensity of the
Creator and Sustainer,* but it would be absurd to claim that in the
same way the Creator and Sustainer cannot in any way go beyond
the totality of the things he made. It is therefore clear that he

8. Anselm discusses the properties of the supreme substance in chapters
13–28 and then resumes discussion of his utterance in chapter 29.

undergirds and transcends, that he encompasses and penetrates all other things. Therefore, if these conclusions are joined to the ones we discovered earlier: it is he who exists in all things and through all things, and from whom and through whom and in whom all things exist.[9]

Chapter 15
What can or cannot be said of him substantially*

Now I am strongly and quite reasonably moved to inquire, as diligently as I can, which of all the things that can be said of something can be applied substantially to such an astounding nature. For I would be amazed if we could find any noun or verb that we apply to things made from nothing that could be appropriately said of the substance that creates all things. Nevertheless, we must try to see what conclusion reason will lead us to in our investigation.

And so with respect to relatives,* at least, no one doubts that none of them is said substantially of the thing of which it is said relatively. Therefore, if something is said relatively of the supreme nature, it does not signify his substance. And so it is clear that whatever can be said of him relatively—the fact that he is supreme among all things, or that he is greater than all the things that he made, or anything else like these—does not designate his natural essence. For if none of those things in relation to which he is said to be supreme or greater had ever existed, he would not be understood as supreme or greater; but he would not on that account be any less good, and his essential greatness would in no way be diminished. This is an obvious conclusion from the fact that he has whatever goodness or greatness he has, not through another, but through himself. So given that the supreme nature can be understood as not supreme and yet as in no way greater or less than when he *is* understood as supreme among all things, it is clear that 'supreme' does not simply signify that essence, who is in every way greater and better than whatever is not what he is. And what reason shows us about 'supreme' is found to be similar in the case of similarly relative terms.

9. Cf. Romans 11:36: "For from him and through him and in him all things exist."

And so, having dismissed those things that are said relatively, since none of them simply refers to the essence of anything, let us turn our attention toward other things that must be discussed. And indeed, if one looks carefully at each of them, whatever there is (other than relatives) is either such that ____ is in every respect better than not-____, or such that not-____ is in some respect better than ____. By "____" and "not-____" here I simply mean true and not-true, body and not-body, and so on.[10]

Now [some things are such that] it is in every respect better to be ____ than not-____, for example, wise than not-wise: that is, it is better to be wise than not-wise. For although a just person who is not wise seems to be better than a wise person who is not just,[11] it is not better in an unqualified* sense to be not-wise than to be wise. Indeed, whatever is not-wise in an unqualified sense, insofar as it is not-wise, is less than what is wise, since everything that is not-wise would be better if it were wise. Similarly, it is in every respect better to be true than not, that is, than not-true, and just than not-just, and living than not-living.

By contrast, [some things are such that] it is in some respect better to be not-____ than to be ____: for example, not-gold than gold. For it is better for a human being to be not-gold than gold, even though perhaps it would be better for something—say, for lead—to be gold than not-gold. For although both a human being and lead are not-gold, a human being is better than gold in proportion as he would be of an inferior nature if he were gold, and lead is baser in proportion as it would be more precious if it were gold.

But many relatives do not fall under this division at all, as is evident from the fact that the supreme nature can be understood as not-supreme, in such a way that supreme is not in every respect better than not-supreme, and not-supreme is not in some respect

---

10. Where I have a blank, Anselm has '*ipsum*', "the very same thing." His point is that you must fill in both blanks with the same word and then apply the test that he explains. If ____ is in every respect better than not-____, then ____ can be said substantially of God. But if not-____ is in some respect better than ____, ____ cannot be said substantially of God. I owe this device to Paul Vincent Spade, trans. and ed., *Five Texts on the Mediaeval Problem of Universals* (Indianapolis: Hackett Publishing Company, 1994), p. 42, where it appears in a somewhat different context.

11. Bear in mind that 'just' here means "morally upright."

better than supreme. I shall not stop to ask whether some relatives do fall under it, since for our present purposes what is already known about them is enough: none of them designates the simple* substance of the supreme nature.

As for everything else, if each is considered individually, either ____ is better than not-____, or not-____ is in some respect better than ____. Therefore, just as it is impious to think that the substance of the supreme nature is something that it is in some way better not to be, so he must be whatever it is in every respect better to be than not to be. For he alone is that than which absolutely nothing else is better, and he alone is better than all things that are not what he is.

Therefore, he is not a body,* or any of the things that the bodily senses perceive. Indeed, there is something better than all of these things that is not what they are. For the rational mind (concerning which no bodily sense perceives what, or what sort of thing, or how great it is) is greater than any of those things that are in the domain of the bodily senses, in proportion as it would be less if it were one of them. For the supreme essence must not at all be said to be any of those things to which something that is not what they are is superior; and, as reason teaches, he absolutely must be said to be any of those things to which whatever is not what they are is inferior. He must therefore be living, wise, powerful and all-powerful, true, just, happy, eternal; and whatever similarly it is absolutely better to be than not to be. Therefore, why should we seek any further for what that supreme nature is, since it is evident which of all things he is, and which he is not?

Chapter 16
That for him, to be just is the same as to be justice, and the same thing holds for those things that can be said of him in a similar way, and that none of these designates what sort of thing or how great he is, but rather what he is[12]

But perhaps when he is said to be just or great or something like that, this does not reveal what he is, but rather what sort of thing

12. For an explanation of Anselm's point in this chapter, see the glossary entry for quality/quantity/quiddity.*

he is or how great he is. For it seems that all these things are said through a quality or a quantity. After all, everything that is just is just through justice, and so on for similar things. Therefore, that supreme nature is just precisely through justice. So it seems that the supremely good substance is said to be just in virtue of his participation in a quality, namely justice. But if that is the case, he is just through another and not through himself.

But that is contrary to the clearly discerned truth that whatever he is—whether good or great or subsistent*—he is through himself and not through another.[13] So given that he is not just except through justice, and he cannot be just except through himself, what is more obvious, what is more necessary, than that this same nature is justice itself; and that when he is said to be just "through justice," this is the same as "through himself"; and that when he is said to be just "through himself," this means nothing other than "through justice"? Therefore, if someone asks, "What is this supreme nature you are discussing?" what truer answer could be given than "Justice"?

So we must see what is meant when that nature, which is justice itself, is said to be just. Now a human being cannot *be* justice, but he can *have* justice. Consequently, a just human being is not understood as existent justice, but rather as having justice. Now the supreme nature cannot properly be said to *have* justice, but rather to *exist as* justice. Therefore, when he is said to be just, he is properly understood as existent justice, not as having justice. Now if, when he is said to be existent justice, this does not express what sort of thing he is, but rather what he is, it follows that when he is said to be just, this too does not express what sort of thing he is, but what he is. Further, since to say of that supreme essence that he is just, is the same as to say that he is existent justice, and to say that he is existent justice is no different from saying that he is justice, there is no difference between saying that he is just and saying that he is justice. Therefore, when someone asks what he is, "Just" is no less fitting an answer than "Justice."

Now reason constrains the intellect to recognize that what we have discovered to be certain in the case of justice applies to all the things that are said of the supreme nature in a similar way. So whichever of them is said of him designates neither what sort of

13. Anselm argues for this claim in chapters 1–4.

thing he is nor how great he is, but rather what he is. Now it is clear that whatever good thing the supreme nature is, he is that supremely. And so he is the supreme essence, supreme life, supreme reason, supreme salvation, supreme justice, supreme wisdom, supreme truth, supreme goodness, supreme greatness, supreme beauty, supreme immortality, supreme incorruptibility, supreme immutability, supreme beatitude, supreme eternity, supreme power, supreme unity, which is none other than supremely being, supremely living, and other similar things.

Chapter 17
That he is simple* in such a way
that all the things that can be said of his essence
are one and the same thing in him,
and none of them can be said substantially of him
except with respect to what he is

What then? If that supreme nature is so many good things, will he not be composed of several* good things? Or are they in fact not several good things, but one good thing signified by several words? For every composite needs the things of which it is composed if it is to subsist, and it owes what it is to them, since whatever it is, it is through them, whereas those things are not through it what they are. And consequently a composite is absolutely not supreme. So then, if that nature is composed of several good things, all these features, which hold true of every composite, must apply to him.

But the whole necessity of truth, which became evident above, destroys and overwhelms such impious falsehood by a clear argument. Therefore, since that nature is in no way a composite and yet is in every way those many good things, it must be that all those things are not several, but one. So each of them is the same as all the others, whether all at once or individually. Thus, when he is said to be justice or essence, those words signify the same thing that the others do, whether all at once or individually. And therefore, just as whatever is said essentially* of the supreme substance is one, so whatever he essentially is he is in one way and under one aspect. For when a human being is said to be body and rational and human, these three things are not said in one way or under one aspect. For he is body according to one, rational according to another, and neither of these individually is the whole of the fact that he is human. By contrast, the supreme essence is in no way like this. Whatever he is in any way, he is in every way and under every aspect. For whatever he in any way essentially is, that is the whole of what he is. Therefore, whatever is truly said of his essence is not understood as expressing what sort of thing or how great he is, but rather as expressing what he is. For whatever is a thing of a certain quality or quantity is something else with respect to what it is, and so it is not simple, but composite.

Chapter 18
That he exists without beginning and without end

So from what time has this so simple nature, the Creator and Sustainer* of all things, existed? And until what time will he continue to exist? Or does he instead exist, not from some time and until some time, but rather without beginning and without end? For if he has a beginning, either he has it from himself or through himself, or he has it from another or through another, or he has it from nothing or through nothing. But through the truth that has already been clearly discerned, it has been established[14] that he in no way exists from another or from nothing, or through another or through nothing. So no beginning was in any way allotted to him through another or from another, or through nothing or from nothing. But he cannot have a beginning from himself or through himself, although he does exist from himself and through himself. For he exists from himself and through himself in such a way that the essence he is through himself and from himself is in no way different from the essence through which and from which he exists. By contrast, whatever begins to exist from something or through something is not in every respect the same as that from which or through which it begins to exist. Therefore, the supreme nature did not begin to exist through himself or from himself. Therefore, since he has no beginning through himself or from himself, or through another or from another, or through nothing or from nothing, he in no way has a beginning.

But neither will he have an end. For if he is going to have an end, he is not supremely immortal and supremely incorruptible. But it

14. In chapters 3, 5, and 6.

has been established that he is supremely both immortal and incorruptible.[15] Therefore, he will not have an end. Moreover, if he is going to have an end, he will perish either willingly or unwillingly. Now surely that by whose will the supreme good perishes is not an unqualified* good. But he himself is a true and unqualified good. Therefore, he who assuredly is the supreme good will not perish voluntarily. But if, on the other hand, he is going to perish unwillingly, then he is not supremely powerful or all-powerful. But the necessity of reason has declared that he is supremely powerful and all-powerful.[16] Therefore, he will not perish unwillingly. And so, if the supreme nature will not have an end either willingly or unwillingly, he will in no way have an end.

Moreover, if that supreme nature has a beginning or end, he is not true eternity, as he was irrefutably found to be above.[17] Further, let anyone who can do so think of this: when did it begin to be true, or when was it not true, that something was going to exist? Or when will it cease to be true, and no longer be true, that something existed in the past? But given that neither of these is conceivable, and both statements cannot be true apart from truth, then it is impossible even to think that truth has a beginning or end. Finally, if truth had a beginning or will have an end, before it came into being it was then true that there was no truth, and after it has ceased to exist, it will then be true that there is no truth. Now nothing can be true apart from truth. So truth existed before truth existed, and truth will exist after truth has ceased to exist—which is an absolute absurdity. So, whether truth is said to have a beginning or end or is understood not to have a beginning or end, truth cannot be confined by any beginning or end. Therefore, the same thing follows with respect to the supreme nature, since he is himself the supreme truth.

Chapter 19
How nothing existed before him and nothing will exist after him

But look how nothing once again arises to trouble us, and whatever reason has taught us thus far, supported by the harmonious

---

15. In chapter 16.
16. Ibid.
17. Ibid.

testimony of truth and necessity, it declares to be nothing. For if the things that were set out earlier are fortified with the defenses of necessary truth, it is not the case that something existed before the supreme essence or that something will exist after him. Therefore, nothing existed before him and nothing will exist after him. For, necessarily, either something or nothing preceded him or will follow him.

Now whoever says that nothing existed before him and nothing will exist after him appears to be saying that there was a time before him when nothing existed, and that there will be a time after him when nothing will exist. Therefore, when nothing existed, he did not exist; and when nothing will exist, he will not exist. So how is it that he did not begin to exist from nothing, and how is it that he will not come to nothing, if he did not yet exist when nothing already existed, and if he will no longer exist when nothing will still exist? Why, then, have we wielded such a weight of arguments, if their work is so easily wrecked by nothing? For if it is concluded that the supreme being both comes after nothing, which preceded him, and gives way to nothing, which will follow him, that which was established above as necessarily true will be destroyed by a worthless nothing.

Do we not instead need to fight against nothing, lest so many constructions of necessary reason be besieged by nothing and the supreme good, who has been sought out and discovered by the light of truth, be lost for nothing? Therefore, rather than allowing a place for nothing either before or after the supreme essence, so that nothing itself reduces to nothing the being who through himself brought into existence that which once was nothing, let it instead be declared (if this is possible) that nothing did not exist before the supreme essence and will not exist after him. For the single expression, "Nothing existed before the supreme essence," gives rise to a twofold meaning. One sense is this: before the supreme essence existed, there was a time when nothing existed. But there is a second meaning: before the supreme essence there was not anything. Thus, if I were to say "Nothing has taught me to fly," I would interpret this either as meaning that nothing itself, which signifies not-anything, has taught me to fly, and so it would be false, or else as meaning that there is not anything that has taught me to fly, which is true.

And so it is the first meaning that generates the absurdity discussed above,[18] and reason utterly rejects it as false. It is the other meaning, by contrast, that is perfectly consistent with our earlier conclusions and is compelled to be true by its whole interconnection with them. Therefore, the statement that nothing existed before him is to be understood in accordance with the second meaning. It should not be interpreted as meaning that there was a time when nothing existed but he did not, but rather as meaning that before him, there was not anything. The same sort of twofold meaning applies to the statement that nothing is going to exist after him.

Therefore, if this interpretation of 'nothing' that I have offered is carefully examined, it is most truly concluded that neither something nor nothing either preceded or will follow the supreme essence, and that nothing existed before it or will follow it. And nonetheless, the solidity of what has already been established is not shaken by any worthless nothing.

Chapter 20
That he exists in every place and time

Now it was concluded above that this creating nature exists everywhere and in all things and through all things,[19] and that, from the fact that he neither came into existence nor will cease to exist, it follows that he always was and is and will be.[20] Nevertheless, I feel the rumblings of a contradiction, which compels me to investigate more carefully where and when he exists. Now the supreme essence exists either everywhere and always, or merely somewhere and sometimes, or nowhere and never; or, as I put it, either in every place or time, or determinately in some, or in none.

But what seems more absurd than this: that he who exists supremely and most truly, exists nowhere and never? So it is false that he exists nowhere or never. Further, since no good thing—indeed, since nothing at all—exists without him, if he exists nowhere and never, then every good thing exists nowhere and

18. That is, in the first paragraph of this chapter.
19. Anselm argues for this claim in chapter 14.
20. Anselm argues for this claim in chapter 18.

never, and absolutely everything exists nowhere and never. Just how false that is, there is no need to say. Therefore, it is also false that he exists nowhere and never.

Therefore, he either exists determinately somewhere and sometimes, or everywhere and always. Now if he exists determinately in some place or time, it is only in that place and time, where and when he exists, that anything can exist. Absolutely no essence exists where and when he does not exist, since without him nothing exists. From this it follows that there is some place and some time where and when nothing at all exists. But since that is false (after all, that place and that time are themselves *something*), the supreme nature cannot exist determinately somewhere or sometimes. And if it is said that through himself he exists determinately at a certain place and time, but through his power he exists wherever and whenever anything exists, that is not true. For since it is evident that his power is nothing other than himself, his power in no way exists apart from him. Therefore, since he does not exist determinately somewhere and sometimes, he must exist everywhere and always—that is, in every place and time.

Chapter 21
That he exists in no place or time

Now if this is so, either he exists as a whole in every place or time, or only part of him does, so that another part exists outside every place and time. But if he partly exists and partly does not exist in every place or time, he has parts, which is false. Therefore, he does not partly exist everywhere and always.

But then how does he exist as a whole everywhere and always? This could be understood in two ways: either he exists as a whole all at once in all places and times and by parts in each individual place and time, or he exists as a whole even in each individual place and time. Now if he exists by parts in each individual place and time, he does not escape the composition and division of parts. And that, as we have found,[21] is altogether foreign to the supreme nature. Therefore, he does not exist as a whole in all

21. In chapter 17.

places and times in such a way that he exists by parts in each individual place or time.

The other possibility remains to be discussed, namely, how the supreme nature exists as a whole *both* in all places and times *and* in each of them individually. This of course can only be the case either all at once or at different times. Now up to this point a single pursuit has been able at once to trail both the argument about place and that about time, since they have followed the same tracks. But at this point they part ways; they seem, as it were, to flee from disputation along disparate paths. They must therefore be investigated in separate discussions. Therefore, we shall first see whether the supreme nature can exist as a whole in individual places either all at once or at different times. Then we shall ask the same question about times.[22]

So, if he exists as a whole in individual places, individual wholes exist in individual places. For just as one place is distinct from another place, in such a way that they are individual places, what exists as a whole in one place is distinct from what at the same time exists as a whole in another place, in such a way that they are individual wholes. For if something exists as a whole in a given place, there is nothing of that thing that does not exist in that place. Now if there is nothing of a thing that does not exist in a given place, then there is nothing of that thing that exists at the same time outside that place. Therefore, if something exists as a whole in a given place, there is nothing of it that exists at the same time outside that place. Now if there is nothing of a thing that exists outside some place, there is nothing of that thing that exists at the same time in some other place. Therefore, if something exists as a whole in a given place, there is nothing of it that exists at the same time in some other place. So if something exists as a whole in a given place, how can that whole exist at the same time in some other place, if nothing of it can exist in any other place?

Therefore, since one whole cannot exist as a whole all at once in individual places, it follows that if anything exists as a whole all at once in distinct places, it exists as individual wholes in individual places. And so if the supreme nature exists as a whole at one

22. That is, whether the supreme nature can exist as a whole at individual times either all at once or at different times.

time in all individual places, there are as many individual supreme natures as there can be individual places, which is an
irrational view to hold. Therefore, he does not exist as a whole at
one time in individual places. On the other hand, if he exists as a
whole in individual places at different times, then as long as he
exists in one place, there is no good and no essence in the other
places, since without him nothing at all exists. But the places
themselves show that this is absurd, since they are not nothing,
but something. And so the supreme nature does not exist as a
whole in individual places at different times. So, if he does not
exist as a whole in individual places either at the same time or at
different times, it is clear that he in no way exists as a whole in all
individual places.

Now we must investigate whether that same supreme nature
exists as a whole at individual times, either all at once or distinctly at
individual times. But how does something exist as a whole at
individual times all at once if those times themselves do not exist all
at once? On the other hand, if he exists as a whole separately and
distinctly at individual times, in the way that a human being exists
as a whole yesterday, today, and tomorrow, then it is correct to say
that he existed and exists and will exist. Therefore, his life, which is
nothing other than his eternity, does not exist as a whole all at once;
instead, it is prolonged by parts through the parts of time.

Now his eternity is nothing other than himself. So it would
follow that the supreme essence is divided into parts in accordance with the distinction of times. For if his life is produced by
means of the flow of times, he has a past, present, and future
along with those times. But what is his life, or the duration of his
existence, other than his eternity? Therefore, since his eternity is
nothing other than his essence (as the argument laid out above[23]
proves beyond doubt), if his eternity has a past, present, and
future, it follows that his essence also has a past, present, and
future. Now what is past is not present or future, and what is
present is not future or past, and what is future is not past or
present. So how will our conclusion survive, which became clear
above[24] by a rational and evident necessity—namely, that the
supreme nature is in no way composite, but instead is supremely

23. In chapters 16 and 17.
24. In chapter 17.

simple* and supremely unchangeable—if he is one thing at one time and something else at another, and if he has parts distributed through time? Or instead, if those earlier conclusions are true—rather, since they are quite clearly true—how are these later conclusions possible?

So neither the creating essence nor his life nor his eternity in any way has a past or a future. For how can it be that he has no present, if he truly exists? But "he existed" signifies the past, and "he will exist" signifies the future. So he never existed and never will exist.[25] Therefore, he does not exist as a whole at individual times either distinctly or all at once.

So if, as I have argued, he does not exist as a whole in all places and times in such a way that he exists as a whole in all of them at once and through his parts in each of them individually, or in such a way that he exists as a whole in each of them individually, it is evident that he in no way exists as a whole in every place or time. And since I have likewise discerned that he does not exist in every place or time in such a way that one part exists in every place and time and another part exists outside every place and time, it is impossible for him to exist everywhere and always. For he cannot at all be understood to exist everywhere and always unless he does so either as a whole or in part.

Now if he does not in any way exist everywhere and always, either he exists determinately in some place or time, or else he exists in no place and time. And I have already shown that he cannot exist determinately in some place or time.[26] Therefore, he exists in no place or time. In other words, he exists nowhere and never. For if he exists at all, he must exist either in every place and time, or in some place or time. And yet, once again, since it is irrefutably established not only that he exists through himself, without beginning and without end,[27] but also that without him nothing exists anywhere or at any time,[28] he must exist everywhere and always.

25. To put Anselm's point somewhat less boldly: "he existed" is never true of God, and "he will exist" is never true of him, since both of those expressions signify temporal categories that do not apply to God.

26. In chapter 20.

27. In chapter 18.

28. In chapter 20.

Chapter 22
How he exists in every place and time
and in no place or time

How, then, will these two conclusions, which are presented as so
contrary but proved as so necessary, be reconciled? Perhaps the
supreme nature exists in place or time in a way that does not
prevent him from existing as a whole all at once in individual
places or times, but so that there are not several* wholes, but only
one whole, and so that his life, which is nothing other than true
eternity, is not divided into past, present, and future. For this law
of place and time seems to constrain only those things that exist in
place or time in such a way that they do not transcend the expanse
of space or the duration of time. Of such things, therefore, it is
most truthfully asserted that one and the same whole cannot exist
as a whole all at once in different places and times; but that
conclusion does not apply with any necessity to things that are not
of that sort.

For it seems correct to say that a thing has a place only if
its quantity is circumscribed by a place that contains it and
contained by a place that circumscribes it, and a thing has a time
only if its duration is somehow bounded by a time that measures
it and measured by a time that bounds it. Therefore, if something
is such that its size or duration is not set against any boundary,
whether by place or by time, no place or time properly applies
to it. For since no place does to it what place does, and no time
does to it what time does, we may reasonably say that no place
is its place and no time is its time. Now if something is seen to
have no place or time, it is certainly shown to be in no way subject to any law of place or time. Therefore, no law of place or time
in any way constrains a nature that no place or time encloses in
any confinement.

Does not every reasonable way of looking at this utterly exclude
the possibility that the creating substance, supreme among all
things—who is necessarily alien to and free from the nature
and law of all the things that he himself made from nothing—
is enclosed in the confines of any place or time, since instead
his power, which is nothing other than his essence, encloses
all the things he made by containing them under himself? And
how is it anything but shameless folly to say that any place

circumscribes the size of the supreme truth, or that any time bounds his duration, since absolutely no greatness or smallness of extension in place or time applies to him?

This, then, is the condition of place and time: whatever is enclosed within their boundaries does not escape being characterized by parts, whether the sort of parts its place receives with respect to size, or the sort its time suffers with respect to duration; nor can it in any way be contained as a whole all at once by different places or times. By contrast, if something is in no way constrained by confinement in a place or time, no law of places or times forces it into a multiplicity of parts or prevents it from being present as a whole all at once in several places or times. And so, since this is the condition of place and time, the supreme substance, who is not enclosed by any confinement of place or time, is undoubtedly not constrained by any of their laws.

Therefore, since an inescapable necessity demands that the supreme essence be present as a whole in every place and time, and since no characteristic of place and time prevents him from being present as a whole in every place and time, he must be present as a whole all at once in each and every place and time. For the fact that he is present in a given place or time does not prevent him from being simultaneously and similarly present in this or that other place or time. Nor does the fact that he existed or exists or will exist mean that something of his eternity has vanished from the present time with the past, which no longer exists; or passes away with the present, which barely exists;[29] or is yet to come with the future, which does not yet exist. For that which in no way confines its existence within place or time is not at all compelled or forbidden by the law of places or times to exist or not to exist anywhere or at any time.

For if that supreme essence is said to exist in a place or a time, even though the very same expression is used both of him and of localized or temporal natures because of our customary way of speaking, there is a different meaning because of the dissimilarity of the things themselves. When it comes to localized or temporal natures, this one expression signifies two things: that they are *present at* the times and places in which they are said to exist, and

29. The present, as Anselm is thinking of it, exists only for a moment, and so it no sooner exists than it passes away.

that they are *contained by* those times and places. But in the case of the supreme essence, only one of these meanings applies, namely, that he is present, not that he is contained by them.

Consequently, if our ordinary way of speaking permitted, it would seem more appropriate to say that he exists *with* a time or place rather than *in* a time or place. For saying that something exists *in* another thing implies more strongly that it is contained than does saying that it exists *with* that thing. And so he is properly said to exist in no place or time, since he is in no way contained by any other thing. And yet he can be said in his own way to exist in every place or time, since whatever else exists is sustained by his presence so that it does not fall into nothingness. He exists in every place and time because he is absent from none; he also exists in none, because he has no place or time. Nor does he receive in himself the distinctions of places or times, such as here or there or somewhere, or now or then or sometime. Nor is it the case that he exists in the fleeting present time that we experience, or that he has existed or will exist in the past or future, since these are proper to circumscribed and changeable things, which he is not. And yet they can in some sense be said of him, since he is present to all circumscribed and changeable things just as if he were circumscribed by the same places and changed by the same times.

And thus it is evident—enough so to dissolve the contradiction that arose earlier—how the supreme essence of all exists everywhere and always, as well as nowhere and never, that is, both in every place and time and in no place or time, according to a harmonious truth understood in different ways.

Chapter 23
How he can be better understood as existing everywhere, rather than as existing in every place

Indeed, since it has been established that the supreme nature does not exist in all places any more than in all existing things, not as if he were contained by them, but because he contains them all by pervading them all, why should he not be said to exist everywhere in the sense that he is understood as existing in all existing things, rather than merely as existing in all places? For the truth of the matter bears out this interpretation, and the proper way of speaking about place in no way prevents it. For we often quite properly use place-words for things that are not places and are not confined within any boundaries of place. For example, I might say "Understanding is there in the soul, where rationality is." 'There' and 'where' are place-words, and yet the soul does not confine anything, and understanding and rationality are not confined, within any boundaries of place. Therefore, the truth of the matter is that the supreme nature would be more aptly said to exist everywhere according to this interpretation, so that he is understood as existing in all existing things rather than merely as existing in all places. And since, as the arguments laid out above show, this cannot be otherwise, he necessarily exists in all existing things in such a way that he exists completely as one and the same whole all at once in each of them individually.

Chapter 24
How he can be better understood as existing always, rather than as existing at every time

It has also been established that this supreme substance exists without beginning and without end,[30] and that he has no past or future, or even a temporal—that is, a fleeting—present such as we experience,[31] since his life or eternity, which is nothing other than himself, is unchangeable and without parts. So when 'always', which seems to designate all of time, is said of him, is it not much more truly understood to signify eternity, which is never unlike itself, rather than the variation of times, which is always in some respect unlike itself?

Now for him, to exist is the same as to live. Therefore, if he is said to exist 'always', this is best understood as meaning that he exists or lives eternally; in other words, that he enjoys illimitable life as a whole, perfectly, and all at once.[32] For his eternity appears to be an illimitable life existing as a whole all at once and perfectly.

30. Anselm argues for this claim in chapter 18.

31. Anselm argues for this claim in chapters 21 and 22.

32. Anselm is here echoing the famous definition of eternity found in Boethius, *Consolation of Philosophy*, Book 5, prose 6: "Eternity is the whole and perfect possession of illimitable life all at once."

For, since it became perfectly clear earlier[33] that this same substance is nothing other than his own life and his own eternity, and
that he is in no way limitable, nor exists otherwise than as a whole
all at once and perfectly, what else is true eternity, which belongs
to him alone, but an illimitable life existing as a whole all at once
and perfectly? For by this alone is it evidently seen that true
eternity exists in that substance alone, who alone has been found
to be not made, but the Maker. For true eternity is understood as
lacking the boundaries of a beginning and an end. But this is not
true of any created thing, as is shown by the very fact that they
were made from nothing.

Chapter 25
That he cannot be changed by any accidents*

But that essence, who has been shown[34] to be in every respect the
same as himself substantially: is he not sometimes different from
himself, at least accidentally? But then how is he supremely unchangeable if he can—I will not say, *be* changeable, but at least *be
understood as* changeable through accidents? And on the other
hand, how is he not subject to accidents, when the very fact that
he is greater than all other natures, and that he is unlike them,
seems to be accidental to him?

But why would susceptibility to certain of those things that are
called accidents be inconsistent with natural immutability, if taking on those accidents causes no change in the substance? And in
fact, among all the things that are called accidents, it is understood
that some—all colors, for example—cannot be present or absent
without some variation in the thing that participates in them. But
there are others—some relations, for example—that are known to
bring about no change at all in the thing of which they are said by
beginning or ceasing to be present in it. For example, it is evident
that I am not taller than, shorter than, equal to, or similar to a
human being who will be born after this year. But once he has
been born, I will be able—without any change on my part—to have
and to lose all these relations with respect to him as he grows or is
changed by various qualities. And so it becomes clear that among

33. In chapter 17.
34. In chapter 17.

the things that are called accidents, some do imply a degree of mutability, whereas others in no way destroy immutability.

Therefore, just as the supreme nature never yields a place in his simplicity for accidents that bring about change, in the same way he does not reject being sometimes described in accordance with those accidents that in no way oppose his supreme immutability. And yet his essence is not subject to any accident by which it can be understood to be changeable. From this it can also be concluded that he is not susceptible of any accident. For surely, those accidents that cause a change in something by beginning or ceasing to be present in it are judged, in virtue of that very effect, to be truly accidents of the thing they change; and by the same token, those that lack a similar effect are perceived to be improperly called accidents. Therefore, just as he is always in every respect the same as himself substantially, so he is never in any respect different from himself, even accidentally. But however things stand with the proper use of the word 'accident', it is undoubtedly true that nothing can be said of the supremely unchangeable nature from which he could be understood to be changeable.

Chapter 26
In what sense he is to be called a substance, and that he is beyond every substance, and uniquely is whatever he is

But if what I have observed about the simplicity of this nature is certain, in what sense is he a substance? For although every substance is capable of taking on an admixture of differences or a change from accidents, his unchangeable purity is altogether inaccessible to admixture or change. Therefore, how will it be the case that he is a substance at all, unless 'substance' is used to mean 'essence',[35] and he is just as much beyond as he is above every substance? For however great the difference is between the being who is through himself whatever he is and makes every other being from nothing, and a being that through another is made

---

35. Anselm's point here is that we cannot call God a substance in the sense in which a substance is distinguished from its accidents. But we can use the word 'substance' as interchangeable with 'essence', in which case God is indeed a substance (that is, an essence or being) that is beyond and above all other substances.

from nothing to be whatever it is, the difference is every bit as
great between the supreme substance and those that are not the
same thing that he is. And since he alone among all natures has
from himself whatever existence he has, without the help of any
other nature, is he not uniquely whatever he is, having nothing in
common with his creatures? Accordingly, if any word is ever
applied to him in common with others, it must undoubtedly be
understood to have a very different meaning.

Chapter 27
That he is not included
in a common classification of substances,
and yet he is a substance and an individual spirit

And so it is established that this substance is not included in any
common classification of substances, since every other nature is
excluded from having an essence in common with him. Indeed,
every substance is classified as either universal or individual. A
universal substance is essentially common to several* substances,
as being-a-man is common to individual men; an individual substance has a universal essence in common with others, as individual men have in common with other individual men the fact that
they are men. So how would someone understand the supreme
nature as being included in this classification of other substances,
since he is neither divided into several substances nor conjoined
with any other through a common essence? Nevertheless, since
he not only most assuredly exists but also exists in the highest way
of all things, and the essence of any given thing is generally called
a substance, surely, if he can worthily be called anything at all,
there is nothing to prevent us from calling him a substance.

Now since we know of no worthier essence than spirit or body,*
and of these, spirit is worthier than body, we must of course
declare that he is a spirit and not a body. But since that spirit can
have no parts, and there cannot be more than one spirit like him,
he is necessarily an altogether individual spirit. For since (as was
established earlier) he is not composed of parts,[36] and he cannot
be understood as capable of being changed by any differences or

36. Anselm argues for this claim in chapter 17.

accidents,[37] it is impossible for him to be divisible by any sort of division.

Chapter 28
That this spirit exists in an unqualified* sense, and creatures do not exist at all compared to him

It seems, therefore, to follow from our earlier conclusions that this spirit, who thus exists in his own wonderfully unique and uniquely wonderful way, is in a certain sense the only thing that exists, whereas all the other things that appear to exist do not exist at all compared to him. For if we look at this carefully, he alone will be seen to exist in an unqualified sense and perfectly and absolutely, whereas all other things nearly do not exist at all, and barely do exist. For because of his unchangeable eternity, it can in no way be said of that spirit because of any alteration that he existed or will exist; instead, he exists in an unqualified sense. Nor does he exist changeably, so that he is now something that at some time he was not or will not be. Nor does he fail to be now what at some other time he was or will be. Rather, whatever he is, he is once and for all, all at once, and illimitably. And since his existence is like this, he is rightly said to exist in an unqualified sense and absolutely and perfectly.

By contrast, all other things exist changeably in some respect, so that at some time they were or will be something that they are not now, or they are now something that at some time they were not or will not be. What they once were no longer exists, and what they will be does not yet exist, and what they are in the fleeting, utterly brief, and barely-existing present barely exists. Therefore, since they exist so changeably, it is not unreasonable to deny that they exist in an unqualified sense and perfectly and absolutely, and to assert that they nearly do not exist, and barely do exist.

Further, all things whatsoever that are different from him came from non-being to being, not through themselves but through another; and as far as their own power goes, they return to non-being unless they are sustained through another. How, then, can it be characteristic of them to exist in an unqualified sense or perfectly or absolutely, rather than barely to exist, or nearly not to

37. Anselm argues for this claim in chapter 25.

exist? And only that ineffable spirit can in no way be understood
to have begun from non-being, or to be capable of undergoing any
degeneration from what he is into non-being; and whatever he is,
he is not through anything other than himself, i.e., through what
he himself is. So is not his existence rightly understood to be the
only unqualified, perfect, and absolute existence?

Now surely that which is thus in an unqualified sense and in
every respect the only perfect, unqualified, and absolute existence
can in a certain sense rightly be said to be the only thing that
exists. And on the other hand, whatever is known through the
above argument as not existing in an unqualified sense or perfectly or absolutely, but instead as barely existing or nearly not
existing, is indeed in a certain sense rightly said not to exist. So
according to this argument, only that Creator Spirit exists, and all
created things do not exist. And yet it is not the case that they
utterly do not exist, since they have been made from nothing by
him who alone exists absolutely.

Chapter 29
That his utterance[38] is the very same thing as himself; and yet they are not two spirits, but one

Now, having examined those things regarding the properties of
the supreme nature that have occurred to me up to this point as I
follow the guidance of reason, I think it is appropriate, if I can do
so, to examine his utterance, by which all things were made.[39]
And although everything I was able to ascertain about it above has
the unbending rigor of reason, the fact that it is proved to be the
very same thing as the supreme spirit himself especially compels
me to discuss that utterance more carefully. For if the supreme
spirit made nothing except through himself, and whatever was

38. His "utterance" is discussed in chapters 10–12.

39. Anselm's discussion in chapters 29–63 is meant to provide a philosophical explication of certain elements of the Christian understanding of God
as a Trinity. Since some of Anselm's points, as well as much of the language
that he uses, will not be fully clear unless the reader already has some
knowledge of Trinitarian doctrine, I have provided the necessary explanations in notes as well as in the Glossary. See the entries for consubstantial*
and Word.*

made by him was made through his utterance, how can that utterance be anything other than what he himself is?

Moreover, the things we have already discovered declare irrefutably that nothing at all ever could or can subsist* other than the creating spirit and what he creates.[40] Now it is impossible for the utterance of that spirit to be included among created things, since every subsistent created thing was made through it, and it could not have been made through itself. Indeed, nothing can be made through itself, since whatever is made is posterior* to that through which it was made, and nothing is posterior to itself. And so, since the utterance of the supreme spirit cannot be a creature, the only remaining possibility is that it is nothing other than the supreme spirit.

Finally, this utterance cannot be understood as anything other than the understanding of that spirit, by which he understands all things. For what is it for him to utter something, in this sense of "uttering," other than to understand it? For unlike a human being, he never fails to utter what he understands. Therefore, if that supremely simple* nature is nothing other than what his understanding is, just as he is the same as what his wisdom is, then it must be that in the same way he is nothing other than what his utterance is. But since it is already evident that the supreme spirit is only one, and in every way individual,[41] his utterance must be consubstantial* with him, so that they are not two spirits, but one.

Chapter 30
That this utterance does not consist of several words, but rather is one Word*

Why, then, should I hesitate over the question I left open earlier, namely, whether this utterance consists in several* words or in one?[42] For if this utterance is consubstantial with the supreme nature in such a way that they are not two, but one spirit, then of course that utterance is supremely simple,* just as the supreme

---

40. Anselm argues for this claim in chapter 7.
41. Anselm argues for this claim in chapter 27.
42. Anselm raised this question in passing in chapter 12.

nature is. Therefore, it does not consist of several words; rather, it is one Word, through whom all things were made.

Chapter 31
That this Word is not a likeness of created things, but the truth of their essence, whereas created things are an imitation of that truth; and which natures are greater and more excellent than others

But behold! It seems to me that a question arises that is not easy and yet should in no way be left unresolved. For all words by which we say things in our mind (that is, think them) are likenesses and images of the things of which they are words. And every likeness or image is more or less true as it imitates more or less the thing of which it is a likeness. So what are we to hold about that Word by whom all things are uttered, and through whom all things were made? Is he, or is he not, a likeness of those things that were made through him? For if he is a true likeness of mutable things, he is not consubstantial* with the supreme immutability, which is false. On the other hand, if he is not an altogether true likeness of mutable things, but merely some sort of likeness, the Word of the supreme truth is not altogether true, which is absurd. But if he has no likeness to mutable things, how is it that they were patterned after him?

But perhaps none of this uncertainty will remain if we understand it in this way. The truth of a human being is said to exist in a living human being, whereas in a painted one there is the likeness or image of that truth. In the same way, the truth of existing is understood to be in the Word, whose essence exists so supremely that in a certain sense it alone exists, whereas in the things that by comparison with him in a certain sense do not exist, and yet have been made something through him and in accordance with him, there is judged to be an imitation of that supreme essence. Thus, the Word of the supreme truth, who himself is also the supreme truth, experiences no gain or loss depending on whether he is more or less like creatures; instead, it must be the case that every created thing is so much greater and more excellent the more it is like him who supremely exists and is supremely great.

For it is perhaps on this basis—no, not perhaps—it is *certainly* on this basis that every intellect judges that natures that are in some way living are more excellent than those that are not living, natures that perceive than those that do not perceive, and rational natures than those that lack reason. For since the supreme nature in his own unique way not merely exists but also lives and perceives and is rational, it is clear that of all existing things, what is in some way living is more like him than what is in no way living; and what in some way knows something, even through a bodily sense, is more like him than what perceives nothing at all; and what is rational is more like him than what is not capable of reason. And by a similar argument it is clear that certain natures exist more greatly or to a lesser degree than others. For just as something exists more excellently by nature if its natural essence is closer to the most excellent nature, so a nature exists more greatly if its essence is more like the supreme essence.

That this also is the case can, I think, be easily established. Suppose one first thinks of a substance that lives and is capable of perception and is rational. Then in thought one takes away its rationality, next its ability to perceive, then its life, and finally the bare existence that is all that remains. Who would not understand that the substance that is thus destroyed a little at a time is gradually brought to exist less and less, and finally not to exist at all? So if these things are taken away one at a time, they lead an essence down to a lesser and lesser existence; but if they are added in an orderly way, they lead it up to a greater and greater existence. So it is evident that a living substance exists more greatly than one that is not living, one that is capable of perception than one that is not capable of perception, and one that is rational than one that is not rational. And so there is no doubt that every essence exists more greatly and is more excellent to the extent that it is more like the essence that supremely exists and is supremely excellent.

And so it is sufficiently clear that in the Word, through whom all things were made, there is no likeness of those things, but rather their true and unqualified* essence. By contrast, in the things that were made there is no unqualified and absolute essence; instead, there is barely an imitation of that true essence. Hence it must be that the Word is not more or less true depending on the likeness of created things; instead, every created nature stands at a higher level of essence and dignity the more it is seen to approach him.

Chapter 32
That the supreme spirit utters himself
by his coeternal Word

But since this is so, how can he, who is the unqualified* truth, be the Word of those things of which he is not a likeness? For every word by which a thing is uttered by the mind is a likeness of that thing. And if he is not the Word of those things that were made through him, in what sense is he a Word? Surely every word is the word of some thing. Furthermore, if there were never any creature, there would be no word of a creature. What then? Are we to conclude that the Word, who is the supreme essence and lacks for nothing, would not exist at all if no creature ever existed? Or perhaps that the supreme essence, which the Word is, would indeed be eternal through his essence, but he would not be a Word if nothing were ever made through him? For there can be no word of something that neither existed, nor exists, nor will exist.

But according to this argument, if no essence other than the supreme spirit ever existed, no word at all would exist in him. If no word ever existed in him, he would not utter anything within himself. Now for him, to utter something is the same as to understand it. So if he did not utter anything within himself, he would not understand anything. If he did not understand anything, it would follow that the supreme wisdom, which is nothing other than that same spirit, would not understand anything, which is utterly absurd. What then? If he did not understand anything, how would he be the supreme wisdom?

But then if nothing existed apart from him, what would he understand? Would he not understand *himself*? Indeed, how can it even be thought that the supreme wisdom at some time fails to understand himself, since the rational mind can remember not only itself but even the supreme wisdom, and can understand both him and itself? For if the human mind were not capable of remembering or understanding either him or itself, it would in no way be able to distinguish itself from non-rational creatures or to distinguish him from all of creation by reasoning silently within itself, as my mind is doing now. Therefore, just as that supreme spirit is eternal, so he eternally remembers and understands himself after the likeness of the rational mind—or rather, not after the likeness of anything; instead, he does so paradigmatically,

and the rational mind does so after his likeness. Now if he understands himself eternally, he utters himself eternally. And if he
utters himself eternally, his Word exists with him eternally.
Therefore, whether he is thought to exist without any other essence existing, or along with other things that exist, his Word,
coeternal with him, must exist with him.

Chapter 33
That by one Word he utters both himself
and what he made

But behold! While I was asking about the Word by which the
Creator utters all the things he made, it was the Word by which he
utters himself, who made all things, that presented itself to me.
Does he utter himself by one Word and the things he makes by
some other Word? Or is the Word by which he utters whatever he
makes the very same as the Word by which he utters himself? For
the Word by which he utters himself must also be the very same
thing that he is, just as was true of the Word by which he utters the
things he made. For even if nothing other than the supreme spirit
ever existed, reason nevertheless compels the conclusion that the
Word by which he utters himself necessarily exists. And so what
is truer than this: that his Word is nothing other than what he
himself is? Therefore, if by a Word that is consubstantial* with
himself he utters both himself and the things he makes, it is
evident that the Word by which he utters himself and the Word by
which he utters creation are one substance. So if there is one
substance, how can there be two Words?

But perhaps the identity of the substance does not compel us to
assert the unity of the Word. For he who utters by means of these
words has the same substance they have, and yet he is not a word.
And of course the Word by which the supreme wisdom utters
himself is most appropriately called his Word according to our
earlier argument, since he bears a perfect likeness to him. For it
cannot be denied by any argument that when the rational mind
understands itself by thinking itself, an image of itself is born in its
thought. Indeed, that very thinking of itself *is* its own image,
formed to its own likeness as by its own impress. For whatever the
mind desires to understand accurately, whether through corporeal imagination or through reason, it tries to impress a likeness of

that thing in its thought, so far as it can. And the more truly it does this, the more truly it thinks of that thing. This fact is of course observed more clearly when the mind thinks of something other than itself, especially when it thinks of some body.* For when I think of someone I know who is absent, the gaze of my thought is formed into an image of him like the one that I committed to memory through the vision of my eyes. This image in thought is the word of the man whom I utter by thinking of him. Therefore, when the rational mind understands itself by thinking itself, it has within itself its own image, born from itself—in other words, its thought of itself, formed to its own likeness as by its own impress—although it is reason alone that can distinguish the mind from this image of itself.[43] This image of the mind is its word.

And so who could deny that in this way, when the supreme wisdom understands himself by uttering himself, he begets a likeness of himself that is consubstantial with himself: that is, his Word? Although nothing fully adequate can properly be said of such a uniquely excellent thing, he is not improperly called his likeness, and in the same way also his image[44] and figure and character.[45] By contrast, the Word by whom he utters creation is not the word of creation in a similar sense at all, since he is not a likeness of creation but rather its paradigmatic essence.[46] It follows, therefore, that he does not utter creation by a word of creation. So if he does not utter creation by a word of creation, by whose word *does* he utter creation? For what he utters, he utters by a word, and a word is the word (that is, the likeness) *of something*. Now if he utters nothing other than himself and creation, he cannot utter anything except by his own Word or by a word of creation. Therefore, if he utters nothing by a word of creation, whatever he utters, he utters by his own Word. Therefore, he utters both himself and whatever he made by one and the same Word.

43. That is, when the mind understands itself, there is no real distinction between the mind and its image of itself. The distinction is a purely conceptual one, one that is made by reason alone.

44. Cf. Colossians 1:15: "He is the image of the invisible God."

45. Cf. Hebrews 1:3: "He is the splendor of his glory and the figure of his substance." The Greek word translated 'figure' is χαρακτήρ ('character').

46. See the argument of chapter 31 for this distinction.

Chapter 34
How he can be seen to utter creation by his own Word

But how can such different things—namely, the creating and the created essence—be uttered by one Word, especially since that Word is coeternal with him who utters it, whereas creation is not coeternal with him? Perhaps it is because he is himself the supreme wisdom and the supreme reason, in which all created things exist. For any work that is made according to a craft always—not only when it is made, but even before it is made and after it is destroyed—exists in that craft as nothing other than the craft itself. Therefore, when that supreme spirit utters himself, he utters all created things. For before they were made, and once they have already been made, and when they are destroyed or in any way changed, they always exist in him, not as what they are in themselves, but as what he himself is. For in themselves they are a changeable essence created according to an unchangeable reason; in him, however, they are that first essence and first truth of existing, and the more they are in any way like him, the more truly and excellently do they exist. And so in this way it can reasonably be asserted that when the supreme spirit utters himself, he also, by one and the same Word, utters whatever was made.

Chapter 35
That whatever was made is life and truth in his Word and knowledge

Now since it has been established that his Word is consubstantial with him and exactly like him, it follows necessarily that all the things that exist in him exist in his Word in just the same way. So whatever was made—whether it is living or non-living, or whatever it is in itself—is, in him, life and truth.[47] And since for the supreme spirit there is no difference between knowing and understanding or uttering, he must know all the things he knows in the same way that he utters or understands them. Therefore, just as all things are life and truth in his Word, so are they also in his knowledge.

47. John 1:3–4, as Anselm read it (following Augustine), says, "All things were made through him [i.e., the Word], and without him was nothing made. That which was made is, in him, life."

Chapter 36
In what an incomprehensible way
he utters or knows the things he made

From this it can be most clearly comprehended that no human knowledge can comprehend how that spirit utters or knows the things that were made. For no one doubts that created substances exist in themselves quite differently from how they exist in our knowledge. After all, in themselves they exist through their own essence, whereas in our knowledge it is not their essences but their likenesses that exist. So it follows that they exist more truly in themselves than in our knowledge to the extent that they exist more truly somewhere through their essence than through their likeness. And it is also clear that every created substance exists more truly in the Word, that is, in the understanding of the Creator, than in itself, to the extent that the creating essence exists more truly than a created essence. So if our knowledge is as much surpassed by created substances as their likeness falls short of their essence,[48] how will the human mind understand what that utterance and that knowledge are like, since they are far higher and truer than created substances?

Chapter 37
That whatever he is with respect to creation,
his Word is also; nevertheless, the two of them
together are not so in more than one way

Now since the arguments above clearly show that the supreme spirit made all things through his Word, did not the Word himself also make all things? For since he is consubstantial with him whose Word he is, he must be the supreme essence. But there is only one supreme essence, who is the only Creator and only origin of all created things. For he alone made all things from nothing, not through another, but through himself. So whatever the supreme spirit makes, his Word also makes, and in the same

---

48. Anselm explains in chapter 62 that what is present in our minds when we think of some external object is not the thing itself (its essence) but merely an image of the thing (its likeness).

way.[49] Therefore, whatever the supreme spirit is with respect to creation, his Word is also, and in the same way. Nevertheless, the two of them together are not so in more than one way, for there is not more than one supreme creating essence. Therefore, just as he is the Creator and origin of things, so also is his Word; and yet they are not two, but one Creator and one origin.

Chapter 38
That one cannot say what they are two *of,* and yet they must be two

And so one must pay close attention to something that is quite unusual in the case of other things but seems to happen in the case of the supreme spirit and his Word. For it is certain that whatever they are in their essence, and whatever they are with respect to creation, is present in each of them individually, and in both of them together, in such a way as to be complete in both and yet not introduce any plurality into the two of them. For although the supreme spirit individually is completely the supreme truth and the Creator, and his Word individually is also the supreme truth and the Creator, nevertheless, the two of them together are not two truths or two Creators.

But although this is so, it is nevertheless in a strange way quite clear that the one whose Word exists cannot be his own Word, and the Word cannot be the one whose Word he is. Thus, in that which signifies either what they are substantially or what they are with respect to creation, they always keep an individual unity; but in virtue of the fact that the supreme spirit does not exist from the Word, whereas the Word exists from him, they admit an ineffable plurality.

Ineffable indeed—for although necessity compels that they be two, there is no way to express what they are two *of.* For even if they can be said to be two equals (or something else like that) in relation to each other, if it is asked what the thing is of which these relatives* are said, one will not be able to answer in the plural, as when two lines are said to be equal or two human beings to be similar. Certainly they are not two equal spirits, or two equal

49. Cf. John 5:19: "For whatever [the Father] made, the Son also makes in the same way."

Creators, or two of anything that signifies either their essence or their relationship to creation. Nor are they two of anything that signifies the distinguishing relationship of one to the other; they are not two Words or two images. After all, the Word's being a Word or image implies a relationship to another: he must be the Word or image *of something*. These are the distinguishing characteristics of the Word, so much so that they cannot in any way be shared by the other. For he whose Word or image he is, is neither an image nor a Word.

So it is established that one cannot express what the supreme spirit and his Word are two *of*,[50] although they must be two because of their individual properties. For it is the distinguishing characteristic of the second that he exists from the first, and it is the distinguishing characteristic of the first that the second exists from him.

Chapter 39
That the Word exists from the supreme spirit by being born

This can, it seems, be expressed in no more familiar terms than by saying that it is the distinguishing characteristic of the second that he is born from the first, and it is the distinguishing characteristic of the first that the second is born from him. For it has certainly been established already[51] that the Word of the supreme spirit does not exist from him in the same way as the things that were made by him, but rather as Creator from Creator, supreme from supreme, and—to express their likeness in the briefest way possible—the very same from the very same, and in such a way that he in no way exists except from him. Therefore, since it is evident that the Word of the supreme spirit exists from him alone in such a way that he bears a perfect likeness to him as offspring to parent, and that he does not exist from him in the sense that he is made by him, he is indeed most appropriately thought of as existing from him by being born. Indeed, if we do not hesitate to say that countless things are born from the things from which they have their existence, even though they bear no likeness, as

50. In chapter 79 Anselm takes up this question again.
51. In chapter 29.

offspring to parent, to the things from which they are said to be born—for we say that hair is born from the head and fruit from a tree, although hair is not like the head and fruit is not like the tree—; if, I say, many such things are not absurdly said to be born, it is as much more fittingly said that the Word of the supreme spirit exists from him by being born, as he more perfectly bears a likeness to him, like that of offspring to parent, by existing from him.

Chapter 40
That most truly he is the parent and the Word his offspring

But if the Word is most appropriately said to be born and is so much like the one from whom he is born, why is he regarded as like him in the way that offspring is like a parent? Should it not rather be asserted that one is parent and the other is off- spring the more truly, the more that the one by himself suffices completely for the birth of the other and he who is born expresses his likeness? For in other things that certainly have a relation- ship of parent to offspring, none of them begets in such a way that it needs no help and is by itself completely sufficient to beget its offspring, and none of them is begotten in such a way that it is exactly like its parent, with no admixture of unlikeness. Therefore, given that the Word of the supreme spirit exists so completely from his essence alone, and is like him in such a unique way, that no other offspring exists so completely from the essence of its parent alone or is so much like its parent, the relationship of parent to offspring certainly seems not to apply to anything so fittingly as it does to the supreme spirit and his Word. Therefore, the distin- guishing characteristic of the supreme spirit is to be most truly parent, and the distinguishing characteristic of the Word is to be most truly offspring.

Chapter 41
That he most truly begets and the Word is begotten

Now this could not be the case unless it were equally true that he most truly begets and the Word is most truly begotten. Therefore,

just as the earlier claim is clearly true, this claim must be absolutely certain. Therefore, the supreme spirit most truly begets and
his Word is most truly begotten.

Chapter 42
That he is most truly begetter and Father, and the other is begotten and Son

At this point I should like to conclude (and perhaps I could) that he
is most truly the Father, while the other is mostly truly the Son.
But I think one should not overlook the question whether they are
more properly called 'Father' and 'Son' or 'Mother' and 'Daughter', since there is no distinction of sex in them. For if it is appropriate to call him 'Father' and his offspring 'Son' because they are
both spirit, why would not a parallel argument show that it is
appropriate for one to be Mother and the other Daughter, since
they are both truth and wisdom?[52] Or is it because in those natures
that do have a distinction of sexes, being a father or son is characteristic of the better sex, whereas being a mother or daughter is
characteristic of the lesser sex? This is indeed naturally the case in
most, but in some it is just the opposite, as in certain kinds of
birds, in which the female sex is always larger and stronger,
whereas the male is smaller and weaker.

But surely the real reason why it is more appropriate for the
supreme spirit to be called Father rather than Mother is that the
first and principal cause of offspring is always in the father. For
since the paternal cause always in some way precedes the mater-
nal, it would be quite incongruous to apply the word 'mother' to
that parent who begets his offspring without any other cause that
either accompanies or precedes him. Therefore, it is most true that
the supreme spirit is the Father of his offspring.

Now given that a son is always more like his father than a daughter is, and nothing is more like another than his offspring is like the
supreme Father, it is most true that this offspring is not a daughter
but a Son. Therefore, just as it is the distinguishing characteristic
of the one that he most truly begets and of the other that he is most
truly begotten, so it is the distinguishing characteristic of the one

---

52. This argument relies on the fact that in Latin the word for 'spirit' is
masculine and the words for 'truth' and 'wisdom' are feminine.

that he is most truly begetter and of the other that he is most truly begotten. And just as the one is most truly parent and the other most truly offspring, so the one is most truly Father and the other most truly Son.

Chapter 43
A reconsideration of what is common to both and the distinguishing characteristics of each

Having discovered so many and so great distinguishing characteristics of each, by which it is proved that there is a marvelous plurality—as ineffable as it is inevitable—in the supreme unity, it seems to me most delightful to reconsider so impenetrable a mystery again and again. For behold, it is impossible for him who begets to be the same as him who is begotten, and for the parent to be the same as the offspring—so much so that it is necessary that the begetter be one thing and the begotten something else, and that the Father be one thing and the Son something else. Nevertheless, it is necessary that he who begets be the same as him who is begotten, and that the parent be the same as the offspring—so much so that it is impossible for the begetter to be other than what the begotten is, and for the Father to be other than what the Son is.

Now the Father is one thing and the Son is another, so much so that it is altogether obvious that they are two; and yet that which they both are is so much one and the same thing that it is completely obscure what they are two *of*. For the Father is one thing and the Son another, so much so that when I speak of both, I see that I have spoken of two things; and yet that which is both Father and Son is so much one and the same thing that I do not understand *what* two things I have spoken of. For although the Father individually is completely the supreme spirit, and the Son individually is completely the supreme spirit, nevertheless, the Father-spirit and the Son-spirit are so much one and the same that the Father and the Son are not two spirits, but one spirit.

Thus, just as the individual distinguishing characteristics of each do not admit of plurality, since they do not belong to both of them, so what is common to both keeps its individual unity, even though it belongs wholly to each. For just as there are not two

fathers or two sons, but one Father and one Son, since their
individual distinguishing characteristics belong to them individually, so there are not two spirits but one, even though the Father is
a complete spirit and the Son is also a complete spirit. In virtue of
their relations they are opposed in such a way that neither takes
on the distinguishing characteristic of the other; in virtue of their
nature they are harmonious in such a way that each always has the
essence of the other. For in virtue of the fact that one is the Father
and the other is the Son, they are so different that the Father is
never called the Son and the Son is never called the Father; and in
virtue of their substance they are so much the same that the
essence of the Son always exists in the Father and the essence of
the Father always exists in the Son. For there are not different
essences, but the same essence, not several* essences, but one
essence of both.

Chapter 44
How one is the essence of the other

Hence, if we say that one is the essence of the other, we are
not straying from the truth but rather emphasizing the supreme
unity and simplicity of their common nature. For if we say that
the Father is the essence of the Son and the Son is the essence
of the Father, we cannot understand this in the same way as
when we talk about the wisdom of a man, through which the man
is wise. For a man cannot be wise through himself; but we do
not mean that the Son exists through the Father and the Father
through the Son, as if one could exist only through the other
in the same way that a man can be wise only through wisdom.
For just as the supreme wisdom is always wise through himself, so also the supreme essence always exists through himself.
Now the Father is completely the supreme essence, and the Son
is also completely the supreme essence. Therefore, the Father
exists completely through himself, and the Son also exists completely through himself, just as each of them is wise through
himself.

For that essence or wisdom which is the Son is no less perfect
simply because he is an essence born of the Father's essence and a
wisdom born of his wisdom. But he would indeed be a less perfect

essence or wisdom if he did not exist through himself or were not wise through himself. For it is in no way contradictory that the Son both subsists* through himself and has being from the Father. For just as the Father has essence and wisdom and life in himself, so that it is not through someone else's but through his own essence that he exists, through his own wisdom that he is wise, and through his own life that he lives, so by begetting the Son he grants the Son to have essence and wisdom and life in himself,[53] so that it is not through someone else's essence, wisdom, and life but through his own that he subsists, is wise, and lives. Otherwise the being of the Father and the Son would not be the same, nor would the Son be equal to the Father. And we saw above[54] quite clearly how false that is.

Therefore, it is not contradictory that the Son both subsists through himself and exists from the Father, since this very power of subsisting through himself is necessarily something he has from the Father. For if some wise man teaches me his wisdom, which I formerly lacked, we would rightly say that he had taught me by means of that very wisdom of his. But although my wisdom would have its being and its wisdom from his wisdom, nonetheless, once it existed it would exist only through its own essence and be wise only through itself. So it is all the more true that the eternal Father's coeternal Son—who has being from the Father in such a way that they are not two essences—subsists, is wise, and lives through himself.

So if we say that the Father is the essence of the Son and the Son is the essence of the Father, this cannot be understood as meaning that either of them can subsist only through the other and not through himself. Rather, in order to indicate that they share the supremely simple and supremely unitary essence, it can be fittingly said and understood that each is the very same as the other in such a way that each has the essence of the other. Now for each of them there is no difference between having an essence and being an essence. And so by this argument, just as each has the essence of the other, each *is* the essence of the other; that is, one has the same being as the other.

53. Cf. John 5:26: "For just as the Father has life in himself, so he has granted the Son also to have life in himself."
54. In chapters 29 and 43.

Chapter 45
That the Son can more appropriately be called the essence of the Father than the Father can be called the essence of the Son; and that similarly the Son is the power and wisdom of the Father, and so on

But although this is true according to the argument we have examined, it is far more fitting to call the Son the essence of the Father than to call the Father the essence of the Son. For since the Father has his essence from no one but himself, it is not completely appropriate to say that he has anyone's essence but his own. By contrast, since the Son has his essence from the Father, and indeed the very same essence that the Father has, he can be most appropriately said to have the essence of the Father.

Now neither of them has his essence otherwise than by *being* that essence. Therefore, just as the Son is much more appropriately understood to have the essence of the Father than the Father to have the essence of the Son, so also the Son can be more fittingly called the essence of the Father than the Father can be called the essence of the Son. For this one expression indicates, with quite pointed brevity, not only that the Son has the same essence as the Father, but also that he has it from the Father. Thus, "the Son is the essence of the Father" means "the Son is an essence no different from the Father's essence; indeed, he is an essence from the Father." In the same way, therefore, the Son is the power, the wisdom or truth, and the justice of the Father, and whatever else belongs to the essence of the supreme spirit.

Chapter 46
How some of the statements expressed in this way can also be understood in another way

Nevertheless, some of the statements that can be expressed and interpreted in this way seem to admit another interpretation—and not an inappropriate one—for the very same statement. For it is clear that the Son is the true Word, that is, the perfect understanding or perfect cognition, knowledge, and wisdom of the whole substance of the Father; in other words, he is that which understands and cognizes and knows and is wise concerning the very essence of the Father. Therefore, if one says that the Son is the understanding, wisdom, knowledge, and cognition or awareness of the Father, in the sense that he understands, is wise concerning, knows, and is aware of the Father, one in no way departs from the truth. Also, the Son can be most appropriately called the truth of the Father, not only in the sense that the truth of the Son is the very same truth as that of the Father, as we have already discussed, but also in the sense that in him is understood not an imperfect imitation but the unadulterated truth of the Father's substance, since he is nothing other than what the Father is.

Chapter 47
That the Son is the understanding of understanding and the truth of truth, and so on for similar attributes

Now if the Father's substance is understanding, knowledge, wisdom, and truth, then, since the Son is the understanding, knowledge, wisdom, and truth of the Father's substance, it follows that he is the understanding of understanding, the knowledge of knowledge, the wisdom of wisdom, and the truth of truth.

Chapter 48
That 'memory' signifies the Father just as 'understanding' signifies the Son; and how the Son is the understanding or wisdom of memory, as well as the memory of the Father and the memory of memory

But what are we to hold about memory? Are we to judge that the Son is the understanding of memory, or the memory of the Father, or the memory of memory? Indeed, since it cannot be denied that the supreme spirit remembers himself, nothing could be more appropriate than to use 'memory' to signify the Father, just as we use 'Word' to signify the Son; for it seems that a word is born from the memory, as is more clearly seen in the case of our own mind. For since the human mind is not always thinking of itself, as it always remembers itself, it is clear that when it does think of itself, its word is born from its memory. Hence it is evident that if it were always thinking of itself, its word would always be born from its memory. For to think of a thing we remember is to utter it in our mind; the word of that thing, then, is that very thought, formed out of our memory after the likeness of the thing. And so from this we can quite clearly understand that his coeternal Word is born from the eternal memory of the supreme substance, who always utters himself, just as he always remembers himself. Therefore, just as the Word is fittingly understood to be an offspring, so the memory is quite appropriately called a parent.

Therefore, if the offspring that is born entirely from the supreme spirit alone is the offspring of his memory, nothing follows more logically than that he is his own memory. For it is not the case that by remembering himself he exists in his own memory as one thing exists in another, in the way that things in the memory of the human mind are not our memory itself. Rather, he remembers himself in such a way that he *is* his own memory.

And so it follows that just as the Son is the understanding or wisdom of the Father, so he is also the understanding or wisdom of the Father's memory. Now whatever the Son is wise about or understands, he likewise also remembers. So the Son is the memory of the Father and the memory of memory, that is, the memory that remembers the Father, who is memory; just as he is also the wisdom of the Father and the wisdom of wisdom, that is, the wisdom that is wise concerning the Father, who is wisdom. And the Son is indeed memory born from memory, just as he is wisdom born from wisdom; but the Father is memory or wisdom born from no one.

Chapter 49
That the supreme spirit loves himself

But behold! As I consider with delight the distinguishing characteristics and the common features of the Father and the Son, I find nothing that brings me greater delight to consider than their affection of mutual love. For how absurd it would be to deny that the supreme spirit loves himself, just as he remembers and understands himself, when even the rational mind can be shown to love itself and him in virtue of the fact that it can remember and understand itself and him! After all, the memory and understanding of a thing is idle and completely useless unless the thing itself is either loved or repudiated as reason requires. Therefore, the supreme spirit loves himself, just as he remembers and understands himself.

Chapter 50
That this love proceeds equally from the Father and the Son

Now to anyone who has reason it is perfectly clear that he does not remember or understand himself because he loves himself; rather, he loves himself because he remembers and understands himself. Furthermore, he cannot love himself unless he remembers and understands himself. For nothing is loved unless it is remembered and understood, and many things are remembered and understood that are not loved. It is therefore evident that the love of the supreme spirit proceeds from him in virtue of the fact that he remembers and understands himself. And since by "the memory of the supreme spirit" we mean the Father and by 'understanding' we mean the Son, it is clear that the love of the supreme spirit proceeds equally from the Father and the Son.

Chapter 51
That each loves himself and the other with an equal love

Now if the supreme spirit loves himself, undoubtedly the Father loves himself, the Son loves himself, and each loves the other, because the Father individually is the supreme spirit, and the Son individually is the supreme spirit, and both together are one spirit, and also because each equally remembers and understands himself and the other. And since what loves or is loved in the Father is exactly the same as what loves or is loved in the Son, it must be that each loves himself and the other with an equal love.

Chapter 52
That this love is as great as the supreme spirit

How great, then, is this love of the supreme spirit, which is thus common to the Father and the Son? If his love of himself is as great as his memory and understanding of himself, and his memory and understanding of himself is as great as his essence (and this cannot be otherwise), then his love is indeed as great as he himself is.

Chapter 53
That this love is the very same thing that the supreme spirit is, and yet together with the Father and the Son he is one spirit

But what can be equal to the supreme spirit other than the supreme spirit? And so this love is the supreme spirit. Furthermore, even if no creature – that is, nothing other than the supreme spirit, who is the Father and the Son – ever existed, the Father and Son would nonetheless love both themselves and each other. And so it follows that this love is nothing other than what the Father and the Son are, namely, the supreme essence. Now since there cannot be more than one supreme essence, what is more necessary than that the Father and the Son and the love of each is one supreme essence? So this love is the supreme wisdom, the supreme truth, the supreme good, and whatever else can be said of the substance of the supreme spirit.

Chapter 54
That this love proceeds as a whole from the Father and as a whole from the Son, and yet he is only one love

We must carefully examine whether there are two loves, one proceeding from the Father and the other from the Son; whether there is one proceeding not as a whole from one, but partly from the Father and partly from the Son; or whether there is neither more than one love, nor just one proceeding partly from each individually, but rather one and the same proceeding as a whole from each individually and from both at once. Now we can undoubtedly resolve this doubtful issue by noticing that he does not proceed from that in virtue of which the Father and the Son are more than one, but rather from that in virtue of which they are one. For the Father and the Son equally send forth so great a good, not from their relations, which are more than one (for the relation of Father is one thing and the relation of Son is another), but from their essence, which admits no plurality. Therefore, just as the Father individually is the supreme spirit and the Son individually is the supreme spirit, and the Father and the Son together are not two spirits, but one, so also the whole love of the supreme spirit emanates from the Father individually and from the Son individually, and what emanates from the Father and the Son together is not two wholes, but one and the same whole.

Chapter 55
That this love is not their son

What then? Since this love has being equally from the Father and the Son, and since it is so much like them that it is in no way unlike them but is in every respect the same as they are, should it be considered their son or offspring? Now as soon as the Word is contemplated he gives most compelling proof that he is the offspring of him from whom he exists, for he bears the unmistakable image of his parent; whereas this love just as openly denies that he is an offspring, since when he is understood to proceed from the Father and the Son, he does not immediately exhibit to one who contemplates him his likeness to him from whom he exists, although the argument we have considered shows that he is indeed in every respect the same as the Father and the Son are.

Furthermore, if he is their offspring, either one of them is his father and the other is his mother, or they are both his father or mother. But all these possibilities seem inconsistent with the truth. For since he does not proceed from the Father any differently than from the Son, the truth will not permit dissimilar words to be used to express the Father's and the Son's relation to him. So it is not the case that one is his father and the other his mother. But no nature provides any example of two things, each of which equally has a complete and altogether identical relationship of father or mother to some one thing. Therefore, it is not the case that both the Father and the Son are the father or mother of the love that emanates from them. And so the claim that this love is their son or offspring does not seem at all consistent with the truth.

Chapter 56
That only the Father is begetter and unbegotten,
only the Son is begotten,
and only the love is neither begotten nor unbegotten

Nevertheless, it seems that this love cannot absolutely be called 'unbegotten' in our common way of speaking, but neither can he be called 'begotten' as properly as the Son. For we are accustomed to say frequently that something is begotten from the thing from which it exists, as when we say that heat or light is begotten from fire, or an effect from its cause.[55] So in this sense the love that comes forth from the supreme spirit can in no way be called unbegotten. But on the other hand, he cannot be called 'begotten' as properly as the Word, since the Word is most truly offspring and Son, whereas it is clear that the love is in no way Son or offspring. And so it can be said—indeed, it ought to be said—that only he whose Word exists is begetter and unbegotten, since he alone is Father and parent and in no way exists from another; that only the Word is begotten, since he alone is Son and offspring; and that only the love of both is neither begotten nor unbegotten, since he is neither Son nor offspring, nor is it the case that he in no way exists from another.

Chapter 57
That this love is uncreated and Creator just as the Father and the Son are, and yet he and they together are not three, but one uncreated and one Creator; and that he can be called the Spirit of the Father and the Son

Now this love is individually the supreme essence, just as the Father and the Son are; and yet the Father, the Son, and the love of both are together not several* but one supreme essence, who alone having been made by no one made all things through nothing other than himself. Therefore, it must be that just as the Father individually and the Son individually are uncreated and Creator, so also this love individually is uncreated and Creator, and yet all three together are not many, but one uncreated and one Creator. And so nothing makes or creates or begets the Father; the Father alone does not make but rather begets the Son; and the Father and the Son equally neither make nor beget, but somehow (if one can put it this way) breathe out[56] their love. For although

55. Of course we do not say things like this in English. The verb *'gigni'*, which I have translated as "to be begotten" in view of its use in Trinitarian theology, is here being used in its wider sense to mean "come to exist."

56. The Latin is *'spirant'*. In Trinitarian theology the Father is said to 'beget' the Son; the Father and Son together are said to 'spirate' the Holy Spirit.

the supremely unchangeable essence does not breathe out in the way we do, nonetheless, it seems there may be no more appropriate expression for the way in which he sends forth his love – which proceeds from him ineffably, not by departing from him, but by existing from him – than "breathing out."

Now if one can say this, then just as the Word of the supreme essence is his Son, so his love can be most fittingly called his Spirit.[57] Granted, he is essentially a spirit just as the Father and Son are. But they are not thought of as the spirit *of* something, since the Father does not exist from another, and the Son is not born from the Father by a breathing-out, as it were. This love, by contrast, is regarded as the Spirit of both, since he wondrously proceeds from both in his own inexpressible way by being breathed out. And because he is the communion of the Father and Son, it seems not unreasonable for him to take as his own distinctive name one that is common to the Father and the Son, if the need for a distinctive name for him so requires. Indeed, if this is done – that is, if this love is distinctively designated by the word 'spirit', which equally signifies the substance of the Father and the Son – it usefully serves to indicate that he is the very same thing that the Father and the Son are, although he has his being from them.

Chapter 58
That just as the Son is the essence or wisdom of the Father in the sense that he has the same essence or wisdom as the Father, so also the Spirit is the essence and wisdom (and similar things) of the Father and the Son

In the same way that the Son is the substance and wisdom and power of the Father in the sense that he has the same essence and wisdom and power as the Father, so also the Spirit of both can be understood to be the essence or wisdom or power of the Father and the Son, since he has exactly the same essence, wisdom, and power that they have.

57. That is, if one can say that he is "breathed out" (*spiratur*), he can appropriately be called the "Spirit" (*Spiritus*).

Chapter 59
That the Father and the Son and their Spirit
exist equally in one another

It is joyous to behold how the Father, the Son, and the Spirit of both exist in each other with such equality that none of them exceeds another. For aside from the fact that each of them is perfectly the supreme essence in such a way that all three together are nevertheless only one supreme essence, which cannot be apart from itself or outside itself or greater or less than itself, the same thing can be proved no less for each of them individually. For the Father exists as a whole in the Son and in their common Spirit, the Son exists in the Father and in that same Spirit, and that Spirit exists in the Father and in the Son, since the memory of the supreme essence exists as a whole in his understanding and in his love, his understanding exists in his memory and in his love, and his love exists in his memory and in his understanding. For indeed the supreme spirit understands and loves his whole memory, remembers and loves his whole understanding, and remembers and understands his whole love. Now by 'memory' we mean the Father, by 'understanding' the Son, and by 'love' the Spirit of both. Therefore, the Father, the Son, and the Spirit of both embrace one another and exist in one another with such equality that none of them is found to exceed another or exist apart from another.

Chapter 60
That none of them needs another in order to remem-
ber, understand, or love, since each individually is
memory and understanding and love and whatever
else is necessarily present in the supreme essence

But as I behold these things, something occurs to me that I think should be most carefully borne in mind. For we must understand the Father as memory, the Son as understanding, and the Spirit as love in such a way that the Father does not need the Son or their common Spirit, the Son does not need the Father or that same Spirit, and the Spirit does not need the Father or the Son. It is not as if the Father can remember through himself alone but can understand only through the Son and love only through the Spirit of himself and the Son; and the Son through himself can only understand, but remembers through the Father and loves through their Spirit; and that Spirit through himself can do nothing but love, but the Father remembers for him and the Son understands for him. For since each of these three is individually the supreme essence and supreme wisdom so completely that each remembers and understands and loves through himself, it must be that none of these three needs another in order to remember or understand or love. For each of them individually is essentially memory and understanding and love, and whatever else is necessarily present in the supreme essence.

Chapter 61
That nevertheless there are not three but one Father, one Son, and one Spirit of both

Here I see a question arise. If the Father is understanding and love just as he is memory, and the Son is memory and love in the same way that he is understanding, and the Spirit of both is no less memory and understanding than he is love, how is it that the Father is not a son and someone's spirit? And why is the Son not a father and someone's spirit? And why is that Spirit not someone's father and someone's son? After all, it was understood that the Father was memory, the Son understanding, and the Spirit of both love.

But this question is not difficult to answer if we consider the truths that reason has already discovered. For the Father is not the son or spirit of another simply because he is understanding and love, since he is not an understanding that is begotten or a love that proceeds from someone; rather, whatever he is, is only the begetter and the one from whom another proceeds. And the Son is not a father or someone's spirit simply because he remembers and loves by himself, since he is not a memory that begets or a love that proceeds from another in the way his own Spirit proceeds; rather, whatever existence he has is only begotten, and it is he from whom the Spirit proceeds. And the fact that he contains his own memory and understanding does not mean that the Spirit is a father or son, since he is not a memory that begets or an understanding that is begotten; rather, whatever he is only proceeds. So what prevents us from concluding that in the supreme essence

there is only one Father, one Son, and one Spirit, not three fathers
or three sons or three spirits?

Chapter 62
How it seems that many sons are born from them

But perhaps what I am now realizing contradicts this assertion.
For there should be no doubt that the Father, the Son, and their
Spirit each utters both himself and the other two, just as each
understands both himself and the other two. Now if this is
so, how is it that there are not as many words in the supreme
essence as there are ones uttering and ones being uttered? For if
several* human beings utter some one thing in their thought,
there appear to be as many words of that thing as there are people
thinking, since a word of that thing exists in the thoughts of each
of them. Similarly, if one human being thinks of several things,
there are as many words in the mind of the thinker as there are
things being thought.

But in a human being's thought, when he thinks of something
that exists outside his mind, the word of the thing that is thought
is not born from the thing itself, since that thing is absent from the
gaze of his thought; rather, the word is born from some likeness or
image of the thing. That likeness or image exists in the memory of
the one thinking; or else perhaps a bodily sense is conveying it
into his mind from some present object right then as he is thinking. In the supreme essence, by contrast, the Father, the Son, and
their Spirit are always present to one another—for, as we have
already seen,[58] each exists in the others no less than in himself—in
such a way that when they utter one another, each one who is
uttered seems to beget his own word, just as when he is uttered by
himself. How is it, then, that the Son, and the Spirit of him and
the Father, beget nothing, if each of them begets his own word
when he is uttered by himself or another? Now however many
words we can prove are born from the supreme substance, by our
earlier argument he must beget that many sons and send forth
that many spirits. And so by this argument it seems that there are
in him not only many fathers, sons, and [spirits] proceeding, but
also other relations.

58. In chapter 59.

Chapter 63
How in him there is only one of one[59]

Now certainly the Father, the Son, and their Spirit—about whom it is already most certain that they truly exist—are not three who utter, even though each of them individually utters. Nor is there more than one thing uttered when each utters himself and the other two. For just as knowledge and understanding are present in the supreme wisdom, even so it is natural for that eternal and immutable knowledge and understanding always to behold as present that which it knows and understands. Now for the supreme spirit there is no difference between uttering something in this sense and beholding it in thought, as it were, just as the utterance of our mind is no different from the thinker's observation. Now the arguments we have already considered have made one thing quite certain: whatever is essentially present in the supreme nature belongs completely to the Father, the Son, and their Spirit individually; and yet if the same thing is said of the three of them together, it does not admit of plurality.[60]

Now it is established that just as knowledge and understanding belong to his essence, even so his knowing and understanding are nothing other than his uttering—that is, his always beholding as present—that which he knows and understands. Furthermore, the Father individually and the Son individually and their Spirit individually know and understand, and yet the three of them together are not several* who know and understand, but one who knows and one who understands. In the same way, therefore, it must be the case that each of them individually utters, and yet the three of them together are not three who utter, but one who utters.

From this we can also clearly recognize that when the three of them are uttered, whether by themselves or by one another, it

59. That is, despite how things looked in the previous chapter, it is not the case that in God there are *many* sons born from *many* divine persons. Rather, in God there is only *one* Son born from *one* divine person (namely, the Father).

60. In other words, for any perfection you choose (call it *p*), if *p* belongs to God essentially, then the Father is fully *p*, the Son is fully *p*, and the Holy Spirit is fully *p*. And yet you cannot say that there are three things that are *p*; there is only one. See the argument in chapter 38.

is not the case that more than one thing is uttered. After all, what is uttered there except their essence? So if that essence is only one, that which is uttered is only one. Therefore, if in them that which utters is one, and that which is uttered is one (for in them there is one wisdom that utters and one substance that is uttered), it follows that there are not several words there, but only one. So although each of them utters himself and all of them utter one another, it is impossible for there to be any Word in the supreme essence other than the one concerning whom it has been established[61] that he is born from him whose Word he is in such a way that he can be called his true image and is truly his Son.

I see in this something wonderful and inexplicable. For behold! Although it is evident that each of them—that is, the Father, the Son, and the Spirit of the Father and the Son—equally utters himself and the other two, and that there is only one Word there, nevertheless, it appears that the Word can in no way be called the Word of all three, but of only one of them. For it has been established that he is the image and Son of him whose Word he is, and obviously he cannot sensibly be called the image or Son of himself or of the Spirit who proceeds from him. For he is not born from himself or from the one who proceeds from him; nor does he by existing imitate himself or the one who proceeds from him. He certainly does not imitate himself, or bear to himself a likeness of existing, since imitation or likeness does not exist in just one thing; it requires more than one. And he does not imitate the Spirit or exist after his likeness, since he does not have his existence from the Spirit; rather, the Spirit has his existence from him. So the only remaining possibility is that he is the Word only of him from whom he is born and thereby has his existence, and after whose perfect likeness he exists.

Therefore, one Father, not several fathers; one Son, not several sons; and one proceeding Spirit, not several proceeding spirits, exist in the supreme essence. So although they are three in such a way that the Father is never the Son or the proceeding Spirit, the Son is never the Father or the proceeding Spirit, and the Spirit of the Father and the Son is never the Father or the Son; and although each individually is so complete that he needs no one,

61. In chapters 33 and 42.

nonetheless, that which they are is so much one that, just as it cannot be said in the plural of each of them individually, so also it cannot be said in the plural of the three of them together. And although each equally utters himself, and all of them equally utter one another, nonetheless there are not several words there, but only one; and that Word is not the Word of each individually or of all of them together, but of only one.

Chapter 64
That although this cannot be explained, it must nevertheless be believed

The mystery of so sublime a thing seems to me to transcend every power of human understanding, and for that reason I think one should refrain from attempting to explain how this is true. After all, I think someone investigating an incomprehensible thing ought to be satisfied if his reasoning arrives at the knowledge that the thing most certainly exists, even if his understanding cannot fathom how it is so. Nor should we withhold any of the certainty of faith from beliefs that are asserted on the basis of necessary proofs and are contradicted by no other argument, simply because, owing to the incomprehensibility of their natural sublimity, they do not yield to explanation. Now what is as incomprehensible, as ineffable, as the one who is above all things? Therefore, if the conclusions we have reached thus far concerning the supreme essence have been asserted on the basis of necessary reasons, their solid certainty is in no way shaken even though the understanding cannot fathom them so as to be able to explain them in words. For if our earlier reflection[62] rationally comprehends that it is incomprehensible how that supreme wisdom knows the things he made, about which we ourselves must know so many things, who will explain how he knows or utters himself, about whom nothing, or scarcely anything, can be known by a human being? Therefore, if in uttering himself the Father generates and the Son is generated, "Who will tell of his generation?"[63]

62. In chapter 36.
63. Isaiah 53:8.

Chapter 65
How a true conclusion has been reached
regarding an ineffable thing

But once again, if the nature of his ineffability is like this—
or rather, since it is indeed like this—how will any of our conclusions concerning the relation of the Father, the Son, and him
who proceeds from them, remain intact? For if that has been
explained by a sound argument, in what way is he ineffable? Or, if
he is ineffable, how can our conclusions be correct? Is it that he
could to some extent be explained, and therefore nothing prevents our conclusions from being true, but since he could not be
thoroughly understood, he is therefore ineffable? But how could
one reply to the point that was made earlier in this very discussion:[64] that the supreme essence is so much above and beyond
every other nature that even if sometimes words are applied to
him that are common to other natures, their meanings are in no
way common? For what meaning did I understand in all the words
I thought, if not the common and familiar one? So if the familiar
meaning of words is foreign to him, none of my reasoning applies
to him. How then is it true that something has been discovered
about the supreme essence if what has been discovered is vastly
different from him?

What then? Is it that in one way something has been discovered
about an incomprehensible thing, and in another way nothing
about it has been fully seen? After all, we often say many things
that we do not properly express as they really are; rather, we
signify through some other thing what we are either unwilling or
unable to express properly, as when we speak in riddles. And we
often do not see something properly as the thing itself actually is,
but through some likeness or image, as when we look at someone's face in a mirror. In this way we do indeed both say and not
say, or both see and not see, one and the same thing. We say and
see through some other thing; we do not say or see through its
own distinctive character.[65]

---

64. In chapter 26.

65. "Distinctive character" represents the Latin '*proprietas*'. The *proprietas*
of a thing is whatever it is *in itself,* by its very nature. Anselm is arguing that
we do not know God by knowing his very nature. We do not have direct

And so by this argument it is perfectly possible for our conclusions thus far about the supreme nature to be true and yet for that nature himself nevertheless to remain ineffable, if we suppose that he was in no way expressed through the distinctive character of his essence, but somehow designated through some other thing. For all the words that seem applicable to that nature do not show him to me through his distinctive character so much as they hint at him through some likeness. For when I think of the meanings of these words I more readily conceive in my mind what I observe in created things than what I understand to transcend all human understanding. For by their meaning they produce something in my mind that is much less than—that is in fact vastly different from—that which my mind is trying to come to understand through their tenuous signification. For the word 'wisdom' does not suffice to show me the one through whom all things were made from nothing and are preserved from nothingness. Nor can the word 'essence' express to me the one who through his unique exaltedness is far above all things and through his natural distinctive character is vastly beyond all things. So this is how it is the case *both* that his nature is ineffable, because words can in no way express him as he is, *and* that if reason can teach us to form any judgment about him through some other thing, as in a riddle, that judgment is not false.

Chapter 66
That through the rational mind one comes closest to knowing the supreme essence

Therefore, since it is evident that nothing about this nature can be perceived through his own distinctive character, but only through something else, it is certain that one comes closer to knowing him through that which is nearer to him because it is more like him. For whatever among created things is shown to be more like him must be more excellent by nature. Hence, because of its greater likeness such a thing gives more help to the investigating mind in coming closer to the supreme truth, and because of its more excellent created essence it more fully teaches what that mind

---

intellectual access to what he is in himself. Instead, whatever we know about God must be inferred indirectly through some likeness.

ought to believe about the Creator. And so there is no doubt that the creating essence is known in a more profound way the more he is investigated through a creature that is closer to him. For the argument already considered above[66] leaves no room for doubt that every essence is like the supreme essence to the extent that it exists.

And so it is evident that just as the rational mind is the only thing among all creatures that can rise up to seek him, it is no less true that the rational mind is the only thing through which the mind itself can best make progress in finding him. For we have already realized that it comes especially close to him through the likeness of its natural essence. So what is more obvious than this: that the more diligently the rational mind tries to come to know itself, the more efficaciously it rises up to know him; and the more it neglects to look upon itself, the more it falls away from seeing him?

Chapter 67
That the mind itself is a mirror and image of him

The mind can therefore most fittingly be said to be like a mirror for itself, in which it might see (if I may put it that way) the image of him whom it cannot see face to face.[67] For if the mind alone among all created things can remember and understand and love itself, I do not see why one would deny that there is in it a true image of that essence who in virtue of remembering, understanding, and loving himself constitutes an ineffable Trinity. Or certainly it proves itself to be more truly his image by the fact that it can remember, understand, and love *him*. For that by which it is greater and more like him is that by which it is recognized as a truer image of him. Now it is altogether impossible to think that the rational creature was naturally given anything so preeminent and so much like the supreme wisdom as its ability to remember and understand and love that which is best and greatest of all things. Therefore, no creature was endowed with anything else that thus displays an image of the Creator.

66. In chapter 31.
67. Cf. 1 Corinthians 13:12: "For now we see in a mirror, in a riddle, but then face to face."

Chapter 68
That the rational creature was made for loving him

And so it seems to follow that the rational creature should strive for nothing else so much as to express through voluntary action this image that has been stamped on it through its natural ability. For aside from the fact that it owes its very existence to the one who created it, if it recognizes that it can do nothing else so preeminent as to remember, understand, and love the supreme good, it will certainly be convinced that it ought to will nothing else so preeminently. For who would deny that whatever better things are in our power should be more in our will?

Furthermore, for the rational nature there is no difference between being rational and being able to discern the just from what is not just, the true from what is not true, the good from what is not good, and the greater good from the lesser good. But this ability is altogether useless for it, and utterly empty, unless it loves or repudiates what it discerns in accordance with the judgment of a true discernment. Hence, it is quite obvious that every rational thing exists in order that it might love something more or less, or reject it altogether, according as its rational discernment judges that the thing is more or less good, or not good at all. So nothing is more evident than that the rational creature was made in order that it might love the supreme essence above all other goods, since he is the supreme good—indeed, that it might love nothing but him or [what it loves] for his sake, since he is good through himself, and nothing else is good except through him.

Now it cannot love him unless it strives to remember and understand him. It is therefore clear that the rational creature ought to devote all its power and will to remembering and understanding and loving the supreme good, for which purpose it knows it has its very existence.

Chapter 69
That a soul that always loves him will at some time truly live happily

Now there is no doubt that the human soul is a rational creature. Therefore, it must have been made in order that it might love the supreme essence. So it must have been made either in order that it might love without end or in order that it might at some time lose this love, whether willingly or by force. But it is impious to suppose that the supreme wisdom made it in order that it might at some time either disdain so great a good or lose him by force even though it wills to hold on to him. So the only remaining possibility is that it was made in order that it might love the supreme essence without end.

Now it cannot do this unless it will always live. Therefore, it has been made in such a way that it will always live if it always wills to do what it was made for. Furthermore, the supremely good and supremely wise and omnipotent Creator caused it to exist in order that it might love him, so it would be utterly absurd for him to cause it not to exist as long as it truly loved him; and he willingly gave life to something that did not love him in order that it might always love him, so it would be utterly absurd for him to take that life away, or to allow it to be taken away, from something that loves him in order that it will, necessarily, not love him—especially since there should be no doubt that he loves every nature that truly loves him. It is therefore evident that its life will never be taken away from a human soul if it always strives to love the supreme life.

So what sort of life will it have? After all, what good is a long life unless it is truly secure against the onslaught of troubles? For if someone as long as he lives is subject to troubles that he either fears or suffers, or else is deceived by a false security, is his life not miserable? By contrast, if someone's life is free from these things, he lives happily. But it is utterly absurd that any nature always leads a miserable life by always loving him who is supremely good and omnipotent. It is therefore clear that the human soul is such that if it preserves what it was made for, it will at some time live happily, truly secure from death itself and from all other troubles.

Chapter 70
That he gives himself as a reward
to the one who loves him

Finally, it can in no way seem to be true that he who is most just and most powerful, who gave being to one that did not love him in order that it might be able to love him, would give no reward to one who loves him perseveringly. For if he gives no reward to one who loves him, he who is most just does not distinguish between one who loves what ought to be supremely loved and one who disdains it; nor does he love one who loves him—either that, or it does no good to be loved by him. But all those things are incompatible with his nature. Therefore, he rewards everyone who loves him perseveringly.

But what does he give as a reward? If he gave a rational essence to nothing in order that it might love him, what will he give to someone who loves him if he does not cease to love? If what serves love is so great, how great is that which repays love? And if such is the support of love, what will the benefit of love be like? For if the rational creature, which is useless to itself without this love, is so eminent among all creatures, surely nothing can be the reward of this love except that which is supereminent among all natures. For the very same good who thus demands to be loved compels the one who loves him no less to desire him. For who loves justice, truth, happiness, and incorruptibility in such a way that he does not also desire to enjoy them? So what will the supreme goodness give as a reward to one who loves and desires him, if not himself? For anything else he might give would not be a reward, since it would not recompense the love, or console the one who loves him, or satisfy the one who desires him. Either that, or if he wills to be loved and desired so that he might give something else as a reward, he does not will to be loved and desired for his own sake, but for the sake of something else. But in that case he does not will that he himself be loved, but rather that something else be loved—which it is impious to think.

Therefore, nothing is truer than this: that every rational soul, if it strives to love and desire the supreme happiness as it ought, at some time perceives him so as to enjoy him. Thus, what it now sees as if "in a mirror, in a riddle," it will then see "face to face."[69] Now it is utterly foolish to doubt whether one will enjoy him without end, since one who enjoys him cannot be tortured by fear or deceived by a false security; nor, having once experienced being without him, could one fail to love him; nor will he abandon one who loves him; nor will there be anything else more powerful than he that might separate them against their will. Therefore, any soul that has once begun to enjoy the supreme happiness will be happy eternally.

Chapter 71
That one who disdains him will be eternally miserable

From this of course it follows that a soul that disdains the love of the supreme good will incur eternal misery. One might say that for such disdain it would be more justly punished if it lost its very existence or life, since it did not use itself for what it was made for; but reason in no way allows that after so great a fault it should receive as its punishment the existence it had before any fault at all.[70] Certainly before it existed it could neither be at fault nor experience punishment. Therefore, if a soul that disdains what it was made for dies, so that it experiences nothing, or is nothing at all, it will be in the same state both when it is most greatly at fault and when it is without any fault; nor would the supremely wise justice distinguish between what is capable of no good and wills no evil, and what is capable of the greatest good and wills the greatest evil. Now it is quite obvious how absurd that is. So nothing could seem more logical, and nothing should be believed more certainly, than this: the human soul was made in such a way that if it disdains to love the supreme essence, it will suffer eternal misery. Thus, just as one who loves him will rejoice in an eternal reward, one who disdains him will suffer under an eternal punishment. And just as the former will experience immutable plenty, so the latter will experience inconsolable poverty.

69. 1 Corinthians 13:12.

70. In other words, non-existence, which is the "existence" the soul had before it was guilty of any fault.

Chapter 72
That every human soul is immortal

But if the soul is mortal, it need not be the case that one who loves him is eternally happy or one who disdains him miserable. Therefore, whether it loves or disdains him whom it was created to love, it must be immortal. But if there are some rational souls that must be judged neither to love him nor to disdain him, as the souls of infants appear to be, what are we to hold about them? Are they mortal or immortal? Undoubtedly all human souls are of the same nature. Therefore, since it is established that some are immortal, it must be the case that every human soul is immortal.

Chapter 73
That it is either always miserable
or at some time truly happy

Now since everything that lives is either never or at some time truly secure from all trouble, it must be no less true that every human soul is either always miserable or at some time truly happy.

Chapter 74
That no soul is unjustly deprived of the supreme
good, and that it should strive after him
with all its might

But I think it is undoubtedly most difficult, if not impossible, for any mortal to be able to comprehend through disputation which souls are to be unhesitatingly judged as so loving him whom they were made for loving that they deserve to enjoy him at some time, and which ones as so disdaining him that they deserve to be deprived of him for ever, and how or by what merit those who apparently can be said neither to love nor to disdain him are assigned to eternal happiness or misery. Nevertheless, one should hold with absolute certainty that the supremely just and supremely good Creator of things does not unjustly deprive any soul of the good for which it was made, and that every human being ought to strive after that good by loving and desiring him with all his heart, and with all his soul, and with all his mind.[71]

Chapter 75
That one ought to hope for the supreme essence

But the human soul could in no way exert itself in this effort if it despaired of being able to attain what it is striving for. Therefore, the hope of success is as necessary to it as persistence in struggling is useful.

Chapter 76
That one ought to believe in him[72]

But one cannot love or hope for what one does not believe. And so it is beneficial for the human soul to believe the supreme essence and those things without which he cannot be loved, so that by believing them it might strive for [*in*] him. I think the same thing can be signified fittingly and more briefly if one says "believe in [*in*] the supreme essence" instead of "by believing to strive for [*in*] the supreme essence." For if someone says that he believes in [*in*] him, he seems to make it quite clear both that he strives unto [*ad*] the supreme essence through the faith he professes and that he believes those things that pertain to this striving. For someone who believes what does not pertain to striving for [*in*] him, or who does not strive unto [*ad*] him in virtue of what he believes, does not appear to believe in [*in*] him. And perhaps it would make no difference whether we say that someone believes "in [*in*] him" or "on [*ad*] him," just as "by believing to strive for [*in*] him" and "by believing to strive unto [*ad*] him" can be regarded as meaning the same thing, except for the fact that whoever comes to him by

71. Cf. Matthew 22:37: "You shall love the Lord your God with all your heart, and with all your soul, and with all your mind."

72. Much of the argument in this chapter turns on the question of which of two prepositions is most suitably used with the verbs '*tendere*' (to strive) and '*credere*' (to believe). Unfortunately in English we have to use *four* different prepositions if we are not to outrage idiom, and the point is thus lost in translation. So in order to show what Anselm is doing, I have indicated the Latin preposition in brackets after each occurrence in the English.

striving unto [*ad*] him will not remain outside him but will abide within him for ever. This is more explicitly and readily signified by saying that one ought to strive "for [*in*] him" rather than "unto [*ad*] him."[73] And so by this argument I think it can be more fittingly said that one ought to believe "in [*in*] him" rather than "on [*ad*] him."

Chapter 77
That one ought to believe equally in the Father, the Son, and their Spirit, both in each individually and in all three together

Therefore one ought to believe equally in the Father, the Son, and their Spirit, both in each individually and in all three together. For the Father, the Son, and their Spirit are each individually the supreme essence, and the Father and the Son along with their Spirit are together one and the same supreme essence, in whom alone every human being ought to believe, since he alone is the end at which they ought to aim through love in their every thought and action. From this it is evident that just as no one can strive for him unless he believes him, so also it does no one any good to believe him unless he strives for him.

Chapter 78
What is a living and what a dead faith

Therefore, with however great a certainty so great a thing is believed, that faith will be useless and like something dead unless through love it is strong and alive. For a faith that is accompanied and attended by love will by no means be idle when it has the opportunity to act; instead, it will exert itself to act quite frequently, which it could not do without love. That this is so can be proved by just this one fact: one who loves the supreme justice cannot disdain anything just or tolerate anything unjust. Therefore, since whatever acts, shows that it has life, without which it could not act, it is not absurd to say that an active faith is living, since it has the life of love without which it would not act, and that an idle faith is not living, since it lacks the life of love with which it

73. Since 'in' suggests the idea of motion *into* something, whereas 'ad' merely suggests the idea of motion *toward* something.

would not be idle. Therefore, if not only one who has lost his sight is called blind, but also one who, though he ought to have it, does not, why cannot faith without love similarly be called dead,[74] not because it has lost its life (that is, its love), but because it does not have what it ought always to have? So, just as a faith that through love is active[75] is recognized as living, a faith that through disdain is idle is proved to be dead. And so it can quite appropriately be said that a living faith believes *in* what it ought to believe in,[76] whereas a dead faith merely believes what it ought to believe.

Chapter 79
What the supreme essence can in a certain sense be said to be three *of*

Behold! Clearly it is beneficial for every human being to believe in an ineffable threefold Unity and unified Trinity. They are indeed one and a Unity in virtue of one essence, but I do not know what it is in virtue of which they are three and a Trinity. For although I can say 'Trinity' because of the Father, the Son, and the Spirit of both, who are three, I cannot express by any one word what it is in virtue of which they are three, as if I were to say [they are a Trinity] in virtue of being three persons in the same way that I would say they are a Unity in virtue of being one substance. For they are not to be thought of as three persons, since whenever there are two or more persons, the persons subsist* separately from each other in such a way that there must be as many substances as there are persons. This is known to be true in the case of human beings, who are as many individual substances as they are persons. Therefore, just as there is not more than one substance in the supreme essence, so also there is not more than one person.[77]

74. Cf. James 2:26: "Faith without action is dead."

75. Cf. Galatians 5:6: "Faith, which through charity is active."

76. Because, as was argued in chapter 76, believing in [*in*] God implies striving for [*in*] God.

77. The standard definition of 'person' was from Boethius, *Contra Eutychem* 4.4–5: "an individual substance of a rational nature." Anselm is arguing that in this sense of the word God cannot be three persons, since if he were, he would be three substances, and therefore three gods.

And so if anyone wishes to talk about this with someone, what will he say the Father, the Son, and the Spirit of both are three *of*, unless perhaps for lack of a strictly appropriate word he is forced to choose one of those words that cannot be said in the plural of the supreme essence in order to signify that which cannot be said by a suitable word? For example, he might say that this wondrous Trinity is one essence or nature and three persons or substances.[78] For these two words are more fittingly chosen to signify the plurality within the supreme essence, since 'person' is said only of an individual rational nature, and 'substance' is principally said of individuals, which especially constitute a plurality. For it is individuals that especially stand under (i.e., underlie) accidents,* and therefore they more properly take the name of 'substance'.[79] Hence it had already become evident above[80] that the supreme essence, which does not underlie any accidents, cannot properly be called a substance unless 'substance' is being used instead of 'essence'.[81] Therefore, by this argument of necessity that supreme and unified Trinity or threefold Unity can be blamelessly called one essence and three persons or three substances.

Chapter 80
That he is Lord of all and rules all and is the only God

It therefore seems—indeed, it is unhesitatingly declared—that that which is called God is not nothing, and that the name 'God' is properly assigned only to this supreme essence. Surely everyone who says that God exists (whether one God or more than one) understands him to be nothing other than a substance that he thinks human beings ought to worship because of his preeminent dignity, and to entreat in any pressing need, beyond every nature that is not God. Now what is as deserving of worship because of his dignity, or as properly the object of prayer for anything at all, as the supremely good and supremely powerful spirit, who is

78. See the glossary entry for substance* (3).

79. See the glossary entry for substance* (2).

80. In chapter 36.

81. See the glossary entry for substance* (1) and (2).

Lord of all and rules all? For just as it has been established[82] that all things were made and are sustained through his supremely good and supremely wise omnipotence, so also it is altogether absurd to suppose that he is not the Lord of the things he made, or that they are ruled by something less powerful or less good or less wise, or even by no reason at all, but merely by the unstable disorder of chance. For it is he alone through whom it goes well for anything, without whom it goes well for nothing, and from whom and through whom and in whom all things exist.[83] Therefore, since he alone is not only the good Creator but also the most powerful Lord and most wise Ruler of all things, it is utterly clear that it is he alone whom all other natures should lovingly worship and worshipfully love with all their power, from whom alone they ought to hope for good things, to whom alone they ought to flee from troubles, to whom alone they ought to pray for anything at all. Truly, therefore, he is not merely God; he is the only God, ineffably three and one.

---

82. In chapter 13.

83. Cf. Romans 11:36: "For from him and through him and in him all things exist."

PROSLOGION

Prologue

After I had published, at the urging of some of my brethren, a short work as a pattern for meditation on the reason of faith, adopting the role of someone who, by reasoning silently to himself, investigates things he does not know, I began to wonder, when I considered that it is constructed out of a chaining together of many arguments, whether it might be possible to find a single argument that needed nothing but itself alone for proof, that would by itself be enough to show that God really exists; that he is the supreme good, who depends on nothing else, but on whom all things depend for their being and for their well-being; and whatever we believe about the divine nature. And so I often turned my thoughts to this with great diligence. Sometimes I thought I could already grasp what I was looking for, and sometimes it escaped my mind completely. Finally, I gave up hope. I decided to stop looking for something that was impossible to find. But when I tried to stifle that thought altogether, lest by occupying my mind with useless speculation it should keep me from things I could actually accomplish, it began to hound me more and more, although I resisted and fought against it. Then one day, when my violent struggle against its hounding had worn me down, the thing I had despaired of finding presented itself in the very clash of my thoughts, so that I eagerly embraced the thought I had been taking such pains to drive away.

Therefore, thinking that what I had rejoiced to discover would please a reader if it were written down, I wrote about it and about a number of other things in the work that follows, adopting the role of someone trying to raise his mind to the contemplation of God and seeking to understand what he believes. Since I had judged that neither this work nor the one I mentioned earlier deserved to be called a book, or to bear the name of an author, and yet I did not think they ought to be sent out without so much as a title by which they might induce someone who came across them to read them, I gave each a title. The first I called "A pattern for meditation on the rational basis of faith"; the second I called "Faith seeking understanding." But since both works had been transcribed under these titles by several readers, I was encouraged by a number of people (especially by Hugo, the Most Reverend Archbishop of Lyons, Apostolic Legate to

France, who commanded me by his apostolic authority) to put my own name on these works. And so, in order to do so more suitably, I named the first *Monologion*, which means a speech made to oneself, and the second *Proslogion*, which means a speech made to another.

Contents

Chapter 1
A rousing of the mind to the contemplation of God

Come now, insignificant mortal. Leave behind your concerns for a little while, and retreat for a short time from your restless thoughts. Cast off your burdens and cares; set aside your labor and toil. Just for a little while make room for God, and rest a while in him. "Enter into the chamber" (Matthew 6:6) of your mind, shut out everything but God and whatever helps you to seek him, and seek him "behind closed doors" (Matthew 6:6). Speak now, my whole heart: say to God, "I seek your face; your face, Lord, do I seek" (Psalm 27:8).

Come now, O Lord my God. Teach my heart where and how to seek you, where and how to find you. Lord, if you are not here, where shall I seek you, since you are absent? But if you are everywhere, why do I not see you, since you are present? Truly "you dwell in unapproachable light" (1 Timothy 6:16). And where is this "unapproachable light"? How am I to approach an unapproachable light? Who will lead me into it, so that I can see you in it? And by what signs am I to seek you? Under what aspect? I have never seen you, O Lord my God; I do not know your face. What shall he do, O Lord Most High? What shall he do, this distant exile from you? What shall your servant do, deeply troubled by his love for you and "banished far from your face" (Psalm 51:11)? He longs to see you, but your face is too far away from him. He desires to approach your presence, but your dwelling is unapproachable. He wants to find you, but he does not know where you are. He aspires to seek you, but he does not know your face. Lord, you are my God, and you are my Lord, but I have never seen you. You have made me and remade me, you have given me every good thing that is mine, and still I do not know you. I was created so that I might see you, but I have not yet done what I was created to do.

How wretched human beings are! They have lost the very thing for which they were created. Hard and terrible was their fall! Alas! Think what they have lost and what they have found; think what they left behind and what they kept. They have lost the happiness for which they were created and found an unhappiness for which they were not created. They left behind the only source of happiness and kept what brings nothing but misery. Once "human beings ate the bread of angels" (Psalm 78:25), for which they now

97

hunger; now they "eat the bread of sorrows" (Psalm 127:2), which once they did not know. Alas for the common lamentation of human beings, the universal outcry of the children of Adam! He was satisfied to the full; we sigh with hunger. He had everything he needed; we go begging. He happily possessed those things and abandoned them in misery; we unhappily do without them and miserably desire them, but alas, we remain empty-handed. Why did he not preserve for us, as he could easily have done, what we so woefully lack? Why did he thus shut us out from the light and cover us with darkness? Why did he take away our life and inflict death upon us? What wretches we are! Think whence we have been cast out, whither we have been driven; thrown down from so great a height, and buried so deep. From our homeland into exile; from the vision of God into our blindness; from the joy of immortality into the bitterness and terror of death. What a wretched change! From such great good into such great evil! O woeful loss, woeful sorrow, all is woeful!

Alas, wretched man that I am, one of the wretched children of Eve, far from the presence of God. What have I undertaken, and what have I accomplished? Where was I heading, and where have I come to? What was I reaching toward, and what do I long for? "I have sought the good" (Psalm 122:9), and "behold, confusion!" (Jeremiah 14:19). I was heading for God but stumbled over myself. I sought rest in my solitude but "found trials and sorrows" (Psalm 116:3) deep within. I wanted to laugh as my mind rejoiced, but I am forced to "cry out as my heart weeps" (Psalm 38:8). Joy was hoped for, but look where the sighs are closing in.

"How long, O Lord?" (Psalm 6:3) "How long, O Lord, will you forget us? How long will you turn your face from us?" (Psalm 13:1). When will you look favorably upon us and hear us? When will you "enlighten our eyes" (Psalm 13:3) and "show us your face"? (Psalm 80:3, 7, 19). When will you give yourself to us again? Look favorably upon us, O Lord; hear us, enlighten us, show yourself to us. Give yourself to us again, that it might go well for us; for without you it goes so badly for us. Take pity upon our toils and strivings after you, for without you we can do nothing. You call us; come to our aid. I beseech you, Lord: let me not sigh in despair, but let me breathe hopefully again. I beseech you, Lord: my heart is made bitter with its desolation; sweeten it with your consolation. I beseech you, Lord: in my hunger I began to seek you; let me not depart from you empty. I have come to you starving; let me not leave unsatisfied. I have come as a beggar to one who is rich, as a pitiful wretch to one who has pity; let me not go back penniless and despised. If indeed "I sigh before I eat" (Job 3:24), grant that I might eat after I sigh. Lord, I am bent double; I can only look down. Raise me up so that I can turn my gaze upwards. "My sins are heaped up over my head" and entangle me; "like a heavy burden" they weigh me down (Psalm 38:4). Extricate me; lift my burdens, "lest like a pit they swallow me up" (Psalm 69:15). Let me look up at your light, whether from afar or from the depths. Teach me how to seek you, and show yourself to me when I seek. For I cannot seek you unless you teach me how, and I cannot find you unless you show yourself to me. Let me seek you in desiring you; let me desire you in seeking you. Let me find you in loving you; let me love you in finding you.

I acknowledge, Lord, and I thank you, that you have created in me this image of you so that I may remember you, think of you, and love you. Yet this image is so eroded by my vices, so clouded by the smoke of my sins, that it cannot do what it was created to do unless you renew and refashion it. I am not trying to scale your heights, Lord; my understanding is in no way equal to that. But I do long to understand your truth in some way, your truth which my heart believes and loves. For I do not seek to understand in order to believe; I believe in order to understand. For I also believe that "Unless I believe, I shall not understand."[1]

Chapter 2
That God truly exists

Therefore, Lord, you who grant understanding to faith, grant that, insofar as you know it is useful for me, I may understand that you exist as we believe you exist, and that you are what we believe you to be. Now we believe that you are something than which nothing greater can be thought. So can it be that no such nature* exists, since "The fool has said in his heart, 'There is no God' " (Psalm 14:1; 53:1)? But when this same fool hears me say "something than

1. Cf. Isaiah 7:9 in the Old Latin version: "Unless you believe, you will not understand." Anselm is here indebted to Augustine, who frequently appealed to this verse in explaining his views on the relationship between faith and reason.

which nothing greater can be thought," he surely understands what he hears; and what he understands exists in his understanding,[2] even if he does not understand that it exists [in reality]. For it is one thing for an object to exist in the understanding and quite another to understand that the object exists [in reality]. When a painter, for example, thinks out in advance what he is going to paint, he has it in his understanding, but he does not yet understand that it exists, since he has not yet painted it. But once he has painted it, he both has it in his understanding and understands that it exists because he has now painted it. So even the fool must admit that something than which nothing greater can be thought exists at least in his understanding, since he understands this when he hears it, and whatever is understood exists in the understanding. And surely that than which a greater cannot be thought cannot exist only in the understanding. For if it exists only in the understanding, it can be thought to exist in reality as well, which is greater. So if that than which a greater cannot be thought exists only in the understanding, then the very thing than which a greater *cannot* be thought is something than which a greater *can* be thought. But that is clearly impossible. Therefore, there is no doubt that something than which a greater cannot be thought exists both in the understanding and in reality.

Chapter 3
That he cannot be thought not to exist

This [being] exists so truly that it cannot even be thought not to exist. For it is possible to think that something exists that cannot be thought not to exist, and such a being is greater than one that can be thought not to exist. Therefore, if that than which a greater cannot be thought can be thought not to exist, then that than which a greater cannot be thought is *not* that than which a greater cannot be thought; and this is a contradiction. So that than which a greater cannot even be thought exists so truly that it cannot be thought not to exist.

2. The word here translated 'understanding' is '*intellectus*'. The text would perhaps read better if I translated it as 'intellect', but this would obscure the fact that it is from the same root as the verb '*intelligere*', 'to understand'. Some of what Anselm says makes a bit more sense if this fact is constantly borne in mind.

And this is you, O Lord our God. You exist so truly, O Lord my God, that you cannot even be thought not to exist. And rightly so, for if some mind could think something better than you, a creature would rise above the Creator and sit in judgment upon him, which is completely absurd. Indeed, everything that exists, except for you alone, can be thought not to exist. So you alone among all things have existence most truly, and therefore most greatly; for whatever else exists has existence less truly, and therefore less greatly. So then why did "the fool say in his heart, 'There is no God,'" when it is so evident to the rational mind that you among all beings exist most greatly? Why indeed, except because he is stupid and a fool?

Chapter 4
How the fool said in his heart
what cannot be thought

But how has he said in his heart what he could not think? Or how could he not think what he said in his heart, since to say in one's heart is the same as to think? But if he really—or rather, *since* he really—thought this, because he said it in his heart, and did not say it in his heart, because he could not think it, there must be more than one way in which something is "said in one's heart" or "thought." In one way, to think a thing is to think the word that signifies that thing. But in another way, it is to understand what the thing is. God can be thought not to exist in the first way, but not at all in the second sense. No one who understands what God is can think that God does not exist, although he may say these words in his heart with no signification at all, or with some peculiar signification. For God is that than which a greater cannot be thought. Whoever understands this properly, understands that this being exists in such a way that he cannot, even in thought, fail to exist. So whoever understands that God exists in this way cannot think that he does not exist.

Thanks be to you, my good Lord, thanks be to you. For what I once believed through your grace, I now understand through your illumination, so that even if I did not want to *believe* that you exist, I could not fail to *understand* that you exist.

Chapter 5
That God is whatever it is better to be than not to be; and that he alone exists through himself, and makes all other things from nothing

Then what are you, Lord God, than which nothing greater can be thought? What are you, if not the greatest of all beings, who alone exists through himself and made all other things from nothing? For whatever is not this is less than the greatest that can be thought, but this cannot be thought of you. What good is missing from the supreme good, through which every good thing exists? And so you are just, truthful, happy, and whatever it is better to be than not to be. For it is better to be just than unjust, and better to be happy than unhappy.

Chapter 6
How God can perceive even though he is not a body*

Now it is better to be percipient, omnipotent, merciful, and impassible* than not. But how can you perceive if you are not a body? How can you be omnipotent if you cannot do everything? How can you be both merciful and impassible? If only corporeal things can perceive, because the senses exist in a body and are directed towards bodies, then how can you perceive? For you are not a body but the highest spirit, which is better than any body.

But if to perceive is just to know, or is aimed at knowledge— for whoever perceives knows according to the appropriate sense, as, for example, we know colors through sight and flavors through taste—then it is not inappropriate to say that whatever in some way knows also in some way perceives. Therefore, Lord, although you are not a body, you are indeed supremely percipient in the sense that you supremely know all things, not in the sense in which an animal knows things through its bodily senses.

Chapter 7
In what sense God is omnipotent even though there are many things he cannot do

But how are you omnipotent if you cannot do everything?[63] And how can you do everything if you cannot be corrupted, or lie, or cause what is true to be false (as, for example, to cause what has been done not to have been done), or many other such things?

Or is the ability to do these things not power but weakness? For someone who can do these things can do what is not beneficial to himself and what he ought not to do. And the more he can do these things, the more power misfortune and wickedness have over him, and the less he has over them. So whoever can do these things can do them, not in virtue of his power, but in virtue of his weakness. So when we say that he "can" do these things, it is not because he has the power to do them, but because his weakness gives something else power over him. Or else it is some other manner of speaking, such as we often use in speaking loosely. For example, we sometimes say 'to be' instead of 'not to be', or 'to do' instead of 'not to do' or 'to do nothing'. For often when someone denies that something exists, we say "It is as you say it is"; but it would seem more correct to say "It is not as you say it is not." Again, we say "This man is sitting just as that man is doing" or "This man is resting just as that man is doing"; but to sit is not to do anything, and to rest is to do nothing. In the same way, then, when someone is said to have the "power" to do or suffer something that is not beneficial to himself or that he ought not to do, by 'power' we really mean 'weakness'. For the more he has this "power," the more power misfortune and wickedness have over him, and the less he has over them. Therefore, Lord God, you are all the more truly omnipotent because you can do nothing through weakness, and nothing has power over you.

3. This chapter is full of word play in the Latin that does not all come across in English. The words for 'power' (*potentia*), 'weakness' (*impotentia*), and various forms of the verb 'can' (*posse*)—also translated here as 'have power'—all share a common stem. And the word for omnipotent (*omnipotens*) means literally "able to do everything" (*omnia potens*).

Chapter 8
How God is both merciful and impassible*

But how are you both merciful and impassible? For if you are
impassible, you do not feel compassion, and if you do not feel
compassion, your heart is not sorrowful out of compassion for
sorrow; and that is what being merciful is.[4] But if you are not
merciful, how is it that you are such a comfort to the sorrowful?

So how, Lord, are you both merciful and not merciful? Is it not
because you are merciful in relation to us but not in relation to
yourself? You are indeed merciful according to what we feel, but
not according to what you feel. For when you look with favor
upon us in our sorrow, we feel the effect [*effectum*] of mercy, but
you do not feel the emotion [*affectum*] of mercy. So you are merciful, because you save the sorrowful and spare those who sin
against you; but you are also not merciful, because you are not
afflicted with any feeling of compassion for sorrow.

Chapter 9
How the one who is completely and supremely just spares the wicked and justly has mercy on them

But how do you spare the wicked if you are completely and
supremely just? For how does the one who is completely and
supremely just do something that is not just? And what sort of
justice is it to give everlasting life to someone who deserves
eternal death? How then, O good God, good to the good and to
the wicked, how do you save the wicked if this is not just and you
do not do anything that is not just?

Or, since your goodness is incomprehensible, does this lie
hidden in the "inaccessible light where you dwell" (1 Timothy
6:16)? It is indeed in the highest and most secret place of your
goodness that the spring is hidden whence the river of your
mercy flows. For although you are totally and supremely just,
you are nonetheless kind even to the wicked, since you are totally
and supremely good. After all, you would be less good if you
were not kind to any wicked person. For one who is good both to
the good and to the wicked is better than one who is good only
to the good, and one who is good to the wicked both in punishing and in sparing them is better than one who is good only

4. In Latin, "sorrowful heart" is *miserum cor*; 'merciful' is *misericors*.

in punishing them. So it follows that you are merciful precisely because you are totally and supremely good. And while it may be easy to see why you repay the good with good and the evil with evil, one must certainly wonder why you, who are totally just and lack for nothing, give good things to your evil and guilty creatures.

O God, how exalted is your goodness! We can see the source of your mercy, and yet we cannot discern it clearly. We know whence the river flows, but we do not see the spring from which it issues. For it is out of the fullness of goodness that you are kind to sinners, while the reason why you are lies hidden in the heights of goodness. True, out of goodness you repay the good with good and the evil with evil, but the very nature of justice seems to demand this. When you give good things to the wicked, however, one knows that he who is supremely good willed to do this, and yet one wonders why he who is supremely just could have willed such a thing.

O mercy, from what rich sweetness and sweet richness you flow forth for us! O immeasurable goodness of God, how intensely ought sinners to love you! You save the just whom justice commends and set free those whom justice condemns. The just are saved with the help of their merits, sinners despite their merits. The just are saved because you look upon the good things you have given them, sinners because you overlook the evil things you hate. O immeasurable goodness that thus "surpasses all understanding" (Philippians 4:7)! Let the mercy that proceeds from your great riches come upon me. Let that which flows forth from you flow over me. Spare me through your mercy, lest you exact retribution through your justice. For even if it is difficult to understand how your mercy coexists with your justice, one must nonetheless believe that it is in no way opposed to justice, because it flows out of your goodness, and there is no goodness apart from justice — indeed, goodness is actually in harmony with justice. In fact, if you are merciful because you are supremely good, and supremely good only because you are supremely just, then you are indeed merciful precisely because you are supremely just. Help me, O just and merciful God, whose light I seek, help me to understand what I am saying. You are indeed merciful because you are just.

So, then, is your mercy born of your justice? Do you spare the wicked because of your justice? If it is so, Lord, if it is so, teach me how it is so. Is it because it is just for you to be so good that you cannot be understood to be better, and to act so powerfully that you cannot be thought to act more powerfully? For what could be more just than this? And this would certainly not be the case if you were good only in punishing and not in sparing, and if you made only those not yet good to be good and did not do this also for the wicked. And so it is in this sense just that you spare the wicked and make them good. And finally, what is not done justly should not be done, and what should not be done is done unjustly. So if it were not just for you to be merciful to the wicked, you should not be merciful; and if you should not be merciful, you would act unjustly in being merciful. But if it is wrong to say this, it is right to believe that you act justly in being merciful to the wicked.

Chapter 10
How God justly punishes and justly spares the wicked

But it is also just for you to punish the wicked. For what could be more just than for the good to receive good things and the wicked bad things? So how is it both just that you punish the wicked and just that you spare the wicked?

Or do you justly punish the wicked in one way and justly spare them in another? For when you punish the wicked, this is just because it accords with their merits; but when you spare the wicked, this is just, not because it is in keeping with their merits, but because it is in keeping with your goodness. In sparing the wicked you are just in relation to yourself but not in relation to us, in the same way that you are merciful in relation to us but not in relation to yourself. Thus, in saving us whom you might justly destroy, you are merciful, not because you experience any emotion, but because we experience the effect of your mercy; and in the same way, you are just, not because you give us our due, but because you do what is fitting for you who are supremely good. And so in this way you justly punish and justly pardon without any inconsistency.

Chapter 11
How "all the ways of the Lord are mercy and truth," and yet "the Lord is just in all his ways"

But is it not also just in relation to yourself, O Lord, for you to punish the wicked? It is certainly just for you to be so just that you cannot be thought to be more just. And you would by no means be so just if you only repaid the good with good and did not repay the wicked with evil. For one who treats both the good and the wicked as they deserve is more just than one who does so only for the good. Therefore, O just and benevolent God, it is just in relation to you both when you punish and when you pardon. Thus indeed "all the ways of the Lord are mercy and truth" (Psalm 25:10), and yet "the Lord is just in all his ways" (Psalm 145:17). And there is no inconsistency here, for it is not just for those to be saved whom you will to punish, and it is not just for those to be condemned whom you will to spare. For only what you will is just, and only what you do not will is not just. Thus your mercy is born of your justice, since it is just for you to be so good that you are good even in sparing the wicked. And perhaps this is why the one who is supremely just can will good things for the wicked. But even if one can somehow grasp why you can will to save the wicked, certainly no reasoning can comprehend why, from those who are alike in wickedness, you save some rather than others through your supreme goodness and condemn some rather than others through your supreme justice.

Thus you are indeed percipient, omnipotent, merciful, and impassible,* just as you are living, wise, good, happy, eternal, and whatever it is better to be than not to be.

Chapter 12
That God is the very life by which he lives, and so on for similar attributes

But clearly, you are whatever you are, not through anything else, but through yourself. Therefore, you are the very life by which you live, the wisdom by which you are wise, and the very goodness by which you are good to the good and to the wicked, and so on for similar attributes.

Chapter 13
How he alone is unbounded and eternal, although other spirits are unbounded and eternal

Everything that is at all enclosed in a place or a time is less than that which is subject to no law of place or time. Therefore, since nothing is greater than you, you are not confined to any place or time; you exist everywhere and always. Since this can be said of you alone, you alone are unbounded and eternal. So how can other spirits also be said to be unbounded and eternal?

And indeed you alone are eternal, because you alone of all beings do not cease to exist, just as you do not begin to exist. But how are you alone unbounded? Is it that a created spirit is bounded compared to you but unbounded compared to a body*? Surely something is completely bounded if, when it is wholly in one place, it cannot at the same time be somewhere else. This is true only of bodies. On the other hand, something is unbounded if it is wholly everywhere at once, and this is true of you alone. But something is both bounded and unbounded if, when it is wholly in one place, it can at the same time be wholly in another place, but not everywhere; and this is true of created spirits. For if the soul were not present as a whole in each part of its body, it would not as a whole sense each part. Therefore, Lord, you are uniquely unbounded and eternal, and yet other spirits are also unbounded and eternal.

Chapter 14
How and why God is both seen and not seen by those who seek him

Have you found what you were seeking, O my soul? You were seeking God, and you have found that he is the highest of all beings, than which nothing better can be thought; that he is life itself, light, wisdom, goodness, eternal happiness and happy eternity; and that he exists always and everywhere. If you have not found your God, how is he the one whom you have found, whom you have understood with such certain truth and true certainty? But if you have found him, why do you not perceive what you have found? Why does my soul not perceive you, O Lord God, if it has found you?

Or has it not found him whom it found to be light and truth? For how did it understand this, if not by seeing that light and truth? Could it have understood anything at all about you except by "your light and your truth" (Psalm 43:3)? Therefore, if it has seen the light and the truth, it has seen you. If it has not seen you, it has not seen the light or the truth. Or perhaps it was indeed the light and the truth that it saw, but it has not yet seen you, because it saw you only in part and did not "see you as you really are" (1 John 3:2).

O Lord my God, you who have fashioned and refashioned me, tell my longing soul what you are besides what it has seen, that it might see purely what it longs to see. It strives to see more, but beyond what it has already seen it sees nothing but darkness. Or rather, it does not see darkness, for "in you there is no darkness" (1 John 1:5); it sees that it cannot see more because of its own darkness. Why is this, Lord, why is this? Is its eye darkened by its own infirmity, or is it dazzled by your splendor? Surely it is both darkened in itself and dazzled by you. Indeed it is both obscured by its own littleness and overwhelmed by your vastness. Truly it is both pinched by its own narrowness and vanquished by your fullness. How great is that light, for from it flashes every truth that enlightens the rational mind! How full is that truth, for in it is everything that is true, and outside it is only nothingness and falsehood! How vast it is, for in one glance it sees all created things, and it sees by whom and through whom and how they were created from nothing! What purity, what simplicity, what certainty and splendor are there! Truly it is more than any creature can understand.

Chapter 15
That God is greater than can be thought

Therefore, Lord, you are not merely that than which a greater cannot be thought; you are something greater than can be thought. For since it is possible to think that such a being exists, then if you are not that being, it is possible to think something greater than you. But that is impossible.

Chapter 16
That this is the "inaccessible light where he dwells"

Truly, Lord, this is the "inaccessible light in which you dwell" (1 Timothy 6:16). For surely there is no other being that can penetrate this light so that it might see you there. Indeed, the reason that I do not see it is that it is too much for me. And yet whatever I do see, I see through it, just as a weak eye sees what it sees by the light of the sun, although it cannot look at that light directly in the sun itself. My understanding cannot see that light.

It is too dazzling; my understanding does not grasp it, and the eye of my soul cannot bear to look into it for long. It is dazzled by its splendor, vanquished by its fullness, overwhelmed by its vastness, perplexed by its extent. O supreme and inaccessible light, O complete and blessed truth, how far you are from me while I am so close to you! How far you are from my sight while I am so present to yours! You are wholly present everywhere, and yet I do not see you. "In you I move and in you I have my being" (Acts 17:28), and yet I cannot come into your presence. You are within me and all around me, and yet I do not perceive you.

Chapter 17
That in God there is harmony, fragrance, savor, softness, and beauty in his own ineffable way

Still, O Lord, you are hidden from my soul in your light and happiness, and so it still lives in its darkness and misery. It looks around, but it does not see your beauty. It listens, but it does not hear your harmony. It smells, but it does not perceive your fragrance. It tastes, but it does not know your savor. It touches, but it does not sense your softness. For you have these qualities in you, O Lord God, in your own ineffable way; and you have given them in their own perceptible way to the things you created. But the senses of my soul have been stiffened, dulled, and obstructed by the long-standing weakness of sin.

Chapter 18
That there are no parts in God or in his eternity, which he himself is

Once again, "behold, confusion!" (Jeremiah 14:19). Behold, once again mourning and sorrow stand in the way of one seeking joy and happiness. My soul hoped for satisfaction, and once again it is overwhelmed by need. I tried to eat my fill, but I hunger all the more. I strove to rise to the light of God, but I fell back down into my own darkness. Indeed, I did not merely fall into it; I find myself entangled in it. I fell before "my mother conceived me" (Psalm 51:5). I was indeed conceived in darkness; I was born enshrouded in darkness. Truly, we all fell long ago in him "in whom we all sinned" (Romans 5:12). In him, who easily possessed it and wickedly lost it for himself and for us, we all lost what we desire to seek but do not know; what we seek but do not find; what we find but is not what we sought. Help me "because of your goodness, O Lord" (Psalm 25:7). "I have sought your face; your face, Lord, will I seek. Turn not your face from me" (Psalm 27:8–9). Lift me up from myself to you. Cleanse, heal, sharpen, "enlighten the eye" (Psalm 13:3) of my soul so that I may look upon you. Let my soul gather its strength, and let it once more strive with all its understanding to reach you, O Lord.

What are you, Lord, what are you? What shall my heart understand you to be? Surely you are life, you are wisdom, you are truth, you are goodness, you are happiness, you are eternity, and you are every true good. These are many things; my narrow understanding cannot see so many things in one glance and delight in all of them at once. How then, Lord, are you all these things? Are they parts of you? Or rather, is not each of them all that you are? For whatever is composed of parts is not completely one. It is in some sense a plurality and not identical with itself, and it can be broken up either in fact or at least in the understanding. But such characteristics are foreign to you, than whom nothing better can be thought. Therefore there are no parts in you, Lord, and you are not a plurality. Instead, you are so much a unity, so much identical with yourself, that you are in no respect dissimilar to yourself. You are in fact unity itself; you cannot be divided by any understanding. Therefore, life and wisdom and the rest are not parts of you; they are all one. Each of them is all of what you are, and each is what the rest are. And since you have no parts, and neither does your eternity, which you yourself are, it follows that no part of you or of your eternity exists at a certain place or time. Instead, you exist as a whole in every place, and your eternity exists as a whole always.

Chapter 19
That God is not in a place or a time, but all things are in him

But if by your eternity you have been, and are, and will be, and if to have been is not the same as to be in the future, and to be is not the same as to have been or to be in the future, then how does your eternity exist as a whole always?

Is it that nothing of your eternity is in the past in such a way that it no longer exists, and nothing is in the future as if it did not exist already? So it is not the case that yesterday you were and tomorrow you will be; rather, yesterday, today, and tomorrow you *are*. In fact, it is not even the case that yesterday, today, and tomorrow you *are*; rather, you *are* in an unqualified* sense, outside time altogether. Yesterday, today, and tomorrow are merely in time. But you, although nothing exists without you, do not exist in a place or a time; rather, all things exist in you. For nothing contains you, but you contain all things.

Chapter 20
That he is before and beyond even all eternal things

Therefore you fill and embrace all things; you are before and beyond all things. And indeed you are before all things, since "before they came into being, you already *are*" (cf. Psalm 90:2). But how are you beyond all things? In what way are you beyond those things that will have no end?

Is it because they can in no way exist without you, whereas you do not exist any less even if they return to nothingness? For in this way you are in a certain sense beyond them. And is it also because they can be thought to have an end, whereas you cannot at all? Thus they do in one sense have an end, but you do not in any sense. And certainly what does not in any sense have an end is beyond what does in some sense come to an end. And do you not also surpass even all eternal things in that both your and their eternity is wholly present to you, whereas they do not yet possess the part of their eternity that is yet to come, just as they no longer possess the part that is past? In this way you are indeed always beyond them, because you are always present somewhere they have not yet arrived—or because it is always present to you.

Chapter 21
Whether this is 'the age of the age'
or 'the ages of the ages'

So is this 'the age of the age' or 'the ages of the ages'?[5] For just as an age of time contains all temporal things, so your eter-

5. That is, is it more correct to identify God's eternity as '*saeculum saeculi*' or as '*saecula saeculorum*'? Both expressions (usually translated into

nity contains even the very ages of time. This eternity is indeed 'an age' because of its indivisible unity, but it is 'ages' because of its boundless greatness. And although you are so great, Lord, that all things are full of you and are in you, nonetheless you have no spatial extension, so that there is no middle or half or any other part in you.

Chapter 22
That he alone is what he is and who he is

Therefore, you alone, Lord, are what you are; and you are who you are. For whatever is one thing as a whole and something else in its parts, and whatever has in it something changeable, is not entirely what it is. And whatever began to exist out of non-existence and can be thought not to exist, and returns to non-existence unless it subsists* through some other being; and whatever has a past that no longer exists and a future that does not yet exist: that thing does not exist in a strict and absolute sense. But you are what you are, since whatever you are in any way or at any time, you are wholly and always that.

And you are the one who exists in a strict and unquali-fied* sense, because you have no past and no future but only a present, and you cannot be thought not to exist at any time. And you are life and light and wisdom and happiness and eternity and many such good things; and yet you are nothing other than the one supreme good, utterly self-sufficient, needing nothing, whom all things need for their being and their well-being.

Chapter 23
That this good is equally Father, Son, and Holy Spirit; and that this is the "one necessary thing," which is the complete, total, and only good

This good is you, O God the Father; it is your Word, that is to say, your Son. For there cannot be anything other than what

---

English as "world without end" or "for ever and ever") were found in Scripture and in the liturgy.

you are, or anything greater or less than you, in the Word by which you utter yourself. For your Word is as true as you are truthful, and therefore he is the same truth that you are and no other. And you are so simple* that nothing can be born of you that is other than what you are. And this good is the one love that is shared by you and your Son, that is, the Holy Spirit, who proceeds from you both. For this love is not unequal to you or to your Son, since you love yourself and him, and he loves himself and you, as much as you and he *are*. Moreover, the one who is equal to both you and him is not other than you and he; nothing can proceed from the supreme simplicity that is other than that from which it proceeds. Thus, whatever each of you is individually, that is what the whole Trinity is together, Father, Son, and Holy Spirit; for each of you individually is nothing other than the supremely simple unity and the supremely united simplicity, which cannot be multiplied or different from itself.

"Moreover, one thing is necessary" (Luke 10:42). And this is that one necessary thing, in which is all good — or rather, which is itself the complete, one, total, and unique good.

Chapter 24
A conjecture as to what sort of good this is, and how great it is

Bestir yourself, O my soul! Lift up your whole understanding, and consider as best you can what sort of good this is, and how great it is. For if particular goods are delightful, consider intently how delightful is that good which contains the joyfulness of all goods — and not such joyfulness as we have experienced in created things, but as different [from that] as the Creator differs from the creature. If created life is good, how good is the life that creates? If the salvation that has been brought about is joyful, how joyful is the salvation that brings about all salvation? If wisdom in the knowledge of created things is desirable, how desirable is the wisdom that created all things from nothing? In short, if there are many and great delights in delightful things, what kind and how great a delight is there in him who made those delightful things?

Chapter 25
What great goods there are for those who enjoy this good

O those who enjoy this good: what will be theirs, and what will not be theirs! Truly they will have everything they want and nothing they do not want. There will be such goods of both body and soul that "neither eye has seen nor ear heard nor the human heart" (1 Corinthians 2:9) conceived. So why are you wandering through many things, you insignificant mortal, seeking the goods of your soul and of your body? Love the one good, in which are all good things, and that is enough. Desire the simple good, which is the complete good, and that is enough. What do you love, O my flesh? What do you long for, O my soul? It is there; whatever you love, whatever you long for, it is there.

If it is beauty that delights you, "the righteous will shine like the sun" (Matthew 13:43). If it is swiftness or strength, or the freedom of a body that nothing can withstand, "they will be like the angels of God" (Matthew 22:30); for "it is sown an animal body, but it will rise a spiritual body" (1 Corinthians 15:44), with a power that is not from nature. If it is a long and healthy life, there is a healthy eternity and eternal health, for "the righteous will live for ever" (Wisdom 5:15) and "the salvation of the righteous is from the Lord" (Psalm 37:39). If it is satisfaction, "they will be satisfied when the glory of God has appeared" (Psalm 17:13). If it is drunkenness, "they will be drunk with the abundance of the house" (Psalm 36:8) of God. If it is music, there the choirs of angels sing unceasingly to God. If it is some pleasure, not impure but pure, God "will give them to drink from the torrent of his pleasure" (Psalm 36:8). If it is wisdom, the very wisdom of God will show itself to them. If it is friendship, they will love God more than themselves and one another as themselves, and God will love them more than they do themselves; for they will love God and themselves and one another through God, and God will love himself and them through himself. If it is concord, everyone will have but one will, for there will be no will among them but the will of God. If it is power, they will be omnipotent through their wills, just as God is through his. For just as God can do what he wills through himself, so they will be able to do what they will through God; for just as they will will only what God wills, so he will will whatever they will—and what he wills cannot fail to be. If it is wealth and honor, God will "set his good and faithful servants over many things" (cf. Matthew 25:21, 23); indeed, they will be called, and will truly be, "sons of God" (Matthew 5:9) and "gods" (Psalm 82:6, John 10:34). Where his Son is, there they too will be, "heirs of God and joint-heirs with Christ" (Romans 8:17). If it is true security, they will be certain that they will never in any way lose this security—or rather, this good; just as certain as they are that they will never give it up voluntarily, and that the loving God will never take it away against their will from those who love him, and that nothing more powerful than God will separate them from God against their will.

What great joy is there where so great a good is present! O human heart, O needy heart, heart that has known troubles, that is indeed overwhelmed by troubles: how greatly would you rejoice if you abounded in all these things! Ask your inmost self whether it can even comprehend its joy at such great happiness. And yet surely if someone else whom you loved in every respect as yourself had that same happiness, your joy would be doubled, for you would rejoice no less for him than for yourself. And if two or three or many more had that same happiness, you would rejoice as much for each of them as you would for yourself, if you loved each one as yourself. Therefore, in that perfect charity of countless happy angels and human beings, where no one will love anyone else less than he loves himself, each one will rejoice for each of the others just as he does for himself. If, then, the human heart will scarcely comprehend its own joy from so great a good, how will it be able to contain so many and such great joys? And indeed, since the more one loves someone, the more one rejoices in his good, it follows that, just as everyone in that perfect happiness will love God incomparably more than himself and all others with him, so everyone will rejoice inconceivably more in God's happiness than in his own, or in that of everyone else with him. But if they love God so much with "their whole heart, mind, and soul" (Matthew 22:37) that their whole heart, mind, and soul are too small for the greatness of their love, they will truly rejoice so much with their whole heart, mind, and soul that their whole heart, mind, and soul will be too small for the fullness of their joy.

Chapter 26
Whether this is the "fullness of joy" that the Lord promises

My God and my Lord, my hope and the joy of my heart, tell my soul whether this is that joy of which you tell us through your Son, "Ask and you shall receive, that your joy may be full" (John 16:24). For I have found a joy that is full and more than full. Indeed, when the heart, the mind, the soul, and the whole human being are filled with that joy, there will still remain joy beyond measure. The whole of that joy will therefore not enter into those who rejoice; instead, those who rejoice will enter wholly into that joy. Speak, Lord; tell your servant inwardly in his heart whether this is the joy into which your servants will enter who "enter into the joy of the Lord" (Matthew 25:21). But surely the joy with which your chosen ones will rejoice is something "no eye has seen, nor ear heard, nor has it entered into the heart of man" (1 Corinthians 2:9). Therefore, Lord, I have not yet expressed or conceived how greatly your blessed ones will rejoice. They will indeed rejoice as much as they love, and they will love as much as they know. How much will they know you then, Lord, and how much will they love you? Truly in this life "eye has not seen, nor has ear heard, nor has it entered into the heart of man" how much they will love and know you in that life.

O God, I pray that I will know and love you that I might rejoice in you. And if I cannot do so fully in this life, I pray that I might grow day by day until my joy comes to fullness. Let the knowledge of you grow in me here, and there let it be full. Let your love grow in me here, and there let it be full, so that my joy here is great in hope, and my joy there is full in reality. O Lord, by your Son you command us—or rather, you counsel us—to ask, and you promise that we will receive, "that our joy may be full." Lord, I ask what you counsel us through our "Wonderful Counselor" (Isaiah 9:6). Let me receive what you promise through your truth, "that my joy may be full." O truthful God, I ask that I may receive, "that my joy may be full." Until then, let my mind ponder on it, my tongue speak of it. Let my heart love it and my mouth proclaim it. Let my soul hunger for it, my flesh thirst for it, my whole being long for it, until I "enter into the joy of my Lord" (Matthew 25:21), who is God, Three in One, "blessed for ever. Amen" (Romans 1:25).

GAUNILO'S REPLY ON BEHALF OF THE FOOL

Someone who either doubts or denies that there is any such nature* as that than which nothing greater can be thought is told that its existence is proved in the following way. First, the very person who denies or entertains doubts about this being has it in his understanding, since when he hears it spoken of he understands what is said. Further, what he understands must exist in reality as well, and not only in the understanding. The argument for this claim goes like this: to exist in reality is greater than to exist only in the understanding. Now if that being exists only in the understanding, then whatever also exists in reality is greater than it. Thus, that which is greater than everything else[6] will be less than something, and not greater than everything else, which is of course a contradiction. And so that which is greater than everything else, which has already been proved to exist in the understanding, must exist not only in the understanding but also in reality, since otherwise it could not be greater than everything else.

He can perhaps reply, "The only reason this is said to exist in my understanding is that I understand what is said. But in the same way, could I not also be said to have in my understanding any number of false things that have no real existence at all in themselves, since if someone were to speak of them I would understand whatever he said? Unless perhaps it is established that this being is such that it cannot be had in thought in the same way that any false or doubtful things can, and so I am not said to think of what I have heard or to have it in my thought, but to understand it and have it in my understanding, since I cannot think of it in any other way except by understanding it, that is, by comprehending in genuine knowledge the fact that it actually exists.

6. Gaunilo regularly says 'maius omnibus', which literally translated is "greater than everything." English idiom demands "greater than everything else," and I have translated it accordingly, but I thought it important to note the discrepancy.

"But first of all, if this were true, there would be no difference in this case between having the thing in the understanding at one time and then later understanding that the thing exists, as there is in the case of a painting, which exists first in the mind of the painter and then in the finished work.

"Furthermore, it is nearly impossible to believe that this being, once someone had heard it spoken of, cannot be thought not to exist, in just the same way that even God can be thought not to exist. For if that were so, why bother with all this argument against someone who denies or doubts that such a nature exists?

"Finally, it must be proved to me by some unassailable argument that this being merely needs to be thought in order for the understanding to perceive with complete certainty that it undoubtedly exists. It is not enough to tell me that it exists in my understanding, since I understand it when I hear about it. I still think I could likewise have any number of other doubtful or even false things in my understanding if I heard them spoken of by someone whose words I understand, and especially if I am so taken in by him that, as often happens, I believe him—as I still do not believe in that being.

"Accordingly, that example of the painter, who already has in his understanding the picture that he is going to paint, is not a close enough analogy to support this argument. For before that picture is painted, it is contained in the craft of the painter, and any such thing in the craft of a craftsman is nothing but a part of his intelligence. For, as Saint Augustine says, 'when a carpenter is about to make a chest in reality, he first has it in his craft. The chest that exists in reality is not a living thing, but the chest that exists in his craft is a living thing, since the soul of the craftsman, in which all those things exist before they are produced, is alive.'⁷ Now how can they be living things in the living soul of the craftsman unless they are nothing other than the knowledge or intelligence of his soul itself? By contrast, except for things that are recognized as belonging to the nature of the mind itself, when the understanding upon hearing or thinking of something perceives that it is true, that truth is undoubtedly distinct from the understanding that grasps it. So even if it is true that there is something than which a greater cannot be thought, that thing, when it is heard

7. *In Iohannem*, tractate 1, n. 17.

and understood, is not the same sort of thing as a picture that exists in the understanding of the painter before it is painted.

"There is a further argument, which I mentioned earlier. When I hear someone speak of that which is greater than everything else that can be thought (which, it is alleged, can be nothing other than God himself), I can no more think of it or have it in my understanding in terms of anything whose genus or species I already know, than I can think of God himself—and indeed, for this very reason I can also think of God as not existing. For I do not know the thing itself, and I cannot form an idea of it on the basis of something like it, since you yourself claim that it is so great that nothing else could be like it. Now if I heard something said about a man I do not know at all, whose very existence is unknown to me, I could think of him in accordance with that very thing that a man is, on the basis of that knowledge of genus or species by which I know what a man is or what men are. Nonetheless, it could happen that the one who spoke of this man was lying, and so the man whom I thought of would not exist. But I would still be thinking of him on the basis of a real thing: not what that particular man would be, but what any given man is.

"But when I hear someone speak of 'God' or 'something greater than everything else,' I cannot have it in my thought or understanding in the same way as this false thing. I was able to think of the false thing on the basis of some real thing that I actually knew. But in the case of God, I can think of him only on the basis of the word. And one can seldom or never think of any truth solely on the basis of a word. For in thinking of something solely on the basis of a word, one does not think so much of the word itself (which is at least a real thing: the sound of letters or syllables) as of the meaning of the word that is heard. And in the present case, one does not do this as someone who knows what is customarily meant by the word and thinks of it on the basis of a thing that is real at least in thought. Instead, one thinks of it as someone who does not know the meaning of the word, who thinks only of the impression made on his mind by hearing the word and tries to imagine its meaning. It would be surprising if one ever managed to reach the truth about something in this way. Therefore, when I hear and understand someone saying that there exists something greater than everything else that can be thought, it is in this way, and this way only, that it is present in my understanding. So much, then, for the claim that that supreme nature already exists in my understanding.

"Then I am offered the further argument that this thing necessarily exists in reality, since if it did not, everything that exists in reality would be greater than it. And so this thing, which of course has been proved to exist in the understanding, would not be greater than everything else. To that argument I reply that if we are to say that something exists in the understanding that cannot even be thought on the basis of the true nature of anything whatever, then I shall not deny that even this thing exists in my understanding. But since there is no way to derive from this the conclusion that this thing also exists in reality, there is simply no reason for me to concede to him that this thing exists in reality until it is proved to me by some unassailable argument.

"And when he says that this thing exists because otherwise that which is greater than everything else would not be greater than everything else, he does not fully realize whom he is addressing. For I do not yet admit—indeed, I actually deny, or at least doubt—that this being is greater than any real thing. Nor do I concede that it exists at all, except in the sense that something exists (if you want to call it 'existence') when my mind tries to imagine some completely unknown thing solely on the basis of a word that it has heard. How, then, is the fact that this greater being has been proved to be greater than everything else supposed to show me that it exists in actual fact? For I continue to deny, or at least doubt, that this has been proved, so that I do not admit that this greater being exists in my understanding or thought even in the way that many doubtful and uncertain things exist there. First I must become certain that this greater being truly exists somewhere, and only then will the fact that it is greater than everything else show clearly that it also subsists* in itself.

"For example, there are those who say that somewhere in the ocean is an island, which, because of the difficulty—or rather, impossibility—of finding what does not exist, some call 'the Lost Island'. This island (so the story goes) is more plentifully endowed than even the Isles of the Blessed with an indescribable abundance of all sorts of riches and delights. And because it has neither owner nor inhabitant, it is everywhere superior in its abundant riches to all the other lands that human beings inhabit.

"Suppose someone tells me all this. The story is easily told and involves no difficulty, and so I understand it. But if this person went on to draw a conclusion, and say, 'You cannot any longer doubt that this island, more excellent than all others on earth, truly exists somewhere in reality. For you do not doubt that this island exists in your understanding, and since it is more excellent to exist not merely in the understanding, but also in reality, this island must also exist in reality. For if it did not, any land that exists in reality would be greater than it. And so this more excellent thing that you have understood would not in fact be more excellent.'—If, I say, he should try to convince me by this argument that I should no longer doubt whether the island truly exists, either I would think he was joking, or I would not know whom I ought to think more foolish: myself, if I grant him his conclusion, or him, if he thinks he has established the existence of that island with any degree of certainty, without first showing that its excellence exists in my understanding as a thing that truly and undoubtedly exists and not in any way like something false or uncertain."

In this way the fool might meet the objections brought against him up to this point. The next assertion is that this greater being is such that even in thought it cannot fail to exist, and that in turn rests entirely on the claim that otherwise this being would not be greater than everything else. To this argument he can make the very same response, and say, "When did I ever say that any such thing as that 'greater than everything else' exists in actual fact, so that on that basis I am supposed to accept the claim that it exists to such a degree that it cannot even be thought not to exist? Therefore, you must first prove by some absolutely incontestable argument that there exists some superior nature,* i.e., one that is greater and better than all others that exist, so that from this we can also prove all of the qualities that that which is greater and better than all other things must necessarily possess." So instead of saying that this supreme thing cannot be *thought* not to exist, perhaps it would be better to say that it cannot be *understood* not to exist, or even to be capable of not existing. For in the strict sense of the word, false things cannot be understood, even though they can of course be thought in the same way that the fool thought that God does not exist.

Furthermore, I know with absolute certainty that I myself exist, but nonetheless I also know that I can fail to exist. But I understand beyond all doubt that the supreme being that exists, namely God, both exists and cannot fail to exist. Now I do not know whether I can think I do not exist even while I know with absolute certainty that I do exist. But if I can, why can I not do the same for anything else that I know with the same certainty? And if I cannot, it is not God alone who cannot be thought not to exist.

The rest of this book is argued so truly, so lucidly and magnificently, full of so much that is useful, and fragrant with the aroma of devout and holy feeling, that it should by no means be belittled on account of the claims made at the beginning, which are indeed accurately understood, but less compellingly argued. Rather, those claims should be demonstrated more solidly, and then the whole book can be accorded great honor and praise.

ANSELM'S REPLY
TO GAUNILO

Since the one who takes me to task is not that fool against whom I was speaking in my book, but a Christian who is no fool, arguing on behalf of the fool, it will be enough for me to reply to the Christian.

You say—whoever you are who say that the fool could say these things—that something than which a greater cannot be thought is in the understanding no differently from that which cannot even be thought according to the true nature of anything at all. You also say that it does not follow (as I say it does) that that than which a greater cannot be thought exists in reality as well simply because it exists in the understanding, any more than it follows that the Lost Island most certainly exists simply because someone who hears it described in words has no doubt that it exists in his understanding. I, however, say this: if that than which a greater cannot be thought is neither understood nor thought, and exists neither in the understanding nor in thought, then either God is not that than which a greater cannot be thought, or else he is neither understood nor thought, and exists neither in the understanding nor in thought. I appeal to your own faith and conscience as the most compelling argument that this is false. Therefore, that than which a greater cannot be thought is indeed understood and thought, and exists in the understanding and in thought. So either the premises by which you attempt to prove the contrary are false, or else what you think follows from them does not in fact follow.

You think that from the fact that something than which a greater cannot be thought is understood, it does not follow that it exists in the understanding; nor does it follow that if it exists in the understanding, it therefore exists in reality. But I say with certainty that if it can be so much as thought to exist, it must necessarily exist. For that than which a greater cannot be thought cannot be thought of as beginning to exist. By contrast, whatever can be thought to exist, but does not in fact exist, can be thought of as beginning to exist. Therefore, it is not the case that that than which a greater cannot be thought can be thought to exist, but does not in fact exist. If, therefore, it can be thought to exist, it does necessarily exist.

Furthermore, if it can be thought *at all*, it necessarily exists. For no one who denies or doubts that something than which a greater cannot be thought exists, denies or doubts that if it did exist, it would be unable to fail to exist either in reality or in the understanding, since otherwise it would not be that than which a greater cannot be thought. But whatever can be thought, but does not in fact exist, could (if it did exist) fail to exist either in reality or in the understanding. So if that than which a greater cannot be thought can be thought at all, it cannot fail to exist.

But let us assume instead that it does not exist, although it can be thought. Now something that can be thought but does not exist, would not, if it existed, be that than which a greater cannot be thought. And so, if it existed, that than which a greater cannot be thought would not be that than which a greater cannot be thought, which is utterly absurd. Therefore, if that than which a greater cannot be thought can be thought at all, it is false that it does not exist—and much more so if it can be understood and can exist in the understanding.

I shall say something more. If something does not exist every-where and always, even if perhaps it does exist somewhere and sometimes, it can undoubtedly be thought not to exist anywhere or at any time, just as it does not exist in this particular place or at this particular time. For something that did not exist yesterday but does exist today can be conceived of as never existing in just the same way that it is understood as not existing yesterday. And some-thing that does not exist here but does exist elsewhere can be thought not to exist anywhere in just the same way that it does not exist here. Similarly, when some parts of a thing do not exist in the same place or at the same time as other parts of that thing, all its parts— and therefore the thing as a whole—can be thought not to exist any-where or at any time. Even if we say that time always exists and that the universe is everywhere, nevertheless, the whole of time does not always exist, and the whole of the universe is not everywhere. And just as each individual part of time does not exist when others do, so each can be thought never to exist. And just as each individ-ual part of the universe does not exist where others do, so each can be thought to exist nowhere. Moreover, whatever is com-posed of parts can, at least in thought, be divided and fail to exist.

Therefore, whatever does not exist as a whole in all places and at all times, even if it does exist, can be thought not to exist. But that than which a greater cannot be thought, if it exists, cannot be thought not to exist. For otherwise, even if it exists, it is not that than which a greater cannot be thought—which is absurd. Therefore, there is no time and no place in which it does not exist as a whole; it exists as a whole always and everywhere.

Do you think the being about whom these things are understood can in any way be thought or understood, or can exist in thought or in the understanding? If it cannot, these claims about it cannot be understood either. Perhaps you will say that it is not understood and does not exist in the understanding because it is not *fully* understood. But then you would have to say that someone who cannot gaze directly upon the purest light of the sun does not see the light of day, which is nothing other than the light of the sun. Surely that than which a greater cannot be thought is understood, and exists in the understanding, at least to the extent that these things about it are understood.

And so I said in the argument that you criticize, that when the fool hears someone utter the words "that than which a greater cannot be thought," he understands what he hears. Someone who does not understand it (if it is spoken in a language he knows) is rather feeble-minded, if indeed he has a mind at all.

Then I said that if it is understood, it exists in the understanding. Or does that which has been shown to exist necessarily in actual fact not exist in any understanding? But you will say that even if it exists in the understanding, it still does not follow that it is understood. Notice, however, that if it is understood, it does follow that it exists in the understanding. For when something is thought, it is thought by means of thinking; and what is thought by means of thinking exists in thinking just as it is thought. And in the same way, when something is understood, it is understood by means of the understanding; and what is understood by means of the understanding exists in the understanding, just as it is understood. What could be clearer than that?

After that I said that if it exists only in the understanding, it can be thought to exist in reality as well, which is greater. Therefore, if it exists only in the understanding, the very same thing is both that than which a greater *cannot* be thought and that than which a greater *can* be thought. Now I ask you, what could be more logical? For if it exists only in the understanding, can it not be thought to exist in reality as well? And if it can, does not the one who thinks it, think something greater than that thing is if it exists only in the understanding? So if that than which a greater *cannot* be thought exists only in the understanding, it is that than which a greater *can* be thought: what more logical conclusion could there be? But of course that than which a greater cannot be thought is not the same in anyone's understanding as that than which a greater can be thought. Does it not follow, therefore, that if that than which a greater cannot be thought exists in any understanding at all, it does not exist only in the understanding? For if it exists only in the understanding, it is that than which a greater can be thought, which is absurd.

But, you say, this is just the same as if someone were to claim that it cannot be doubted that a certain island in the ocean, surpassing all other lands in its fertility (which, from the difficulty—or rather, impossibility—of finding what does not exist, is called "the Lost Island"), truly exists in reality, because someone can easily understand it when it is described to him in words. I say quite confidently that if anyone can find for me something existing either in reality or only in thought to which he can apply this inference in my argument, besides that than which a greater cannot be thought, I will find and give to him that Lost Island, never to be lost again. In fact, however, it has already become quite clear that that than which a greater cannot be thought cannot be thought not to exist, since its existence is a matter of such certain truth. For otherwise it would not exist at all.

Finally, if someone says that he thinks it does not exist, I say that when he thinks this, either he is thinking something than which a greater cannot be thought, or he is not. If he is not, then he is not thinking that it does not exist, since he is not thinking it at all. But if he is, he is surely thinking something that cannot be thought not to exist. For if it could be thought not to exist, it could be thought to have a beginning and an end, which is impossible. Therefore, someone who is thinking it, is thinking something that cannot be thought not to exist. And of course someone who is thinking this does not think that that very thing does not exist. Otherwise he would be thinking something that cannot be thought. Therefore, that than which a greater cannot be thought cannot be thought not to exist.

When I say that this supreme being cannot be *thought* not to exist, you reply that it would perhaps be better to say that it cannot be *understood* not to exist, or even to be capable of not existing. But in fact it was more correct to say that it cannot be *thought* not to exist. For if I had said that this thing cannot be understood not to exist, you (who say that in the strict sense of the word false things cannot be understood) might well object that nothing that exists can be understood not to exist, since, after all, it is false that something that exists does not exist. Consequently, it is not God alone who cannot be understood not to exist. But if any of those things that most certainly exist can be understood not to exist, then other things that are certain can likewise be understood not to exist. If, however, we say 'thought' [rather than 'understood'] this objection will have no force if it is examined properly. For even if nothing that actually exists can be *understood* not to exist, everything can be *thought* not to exist, except for that which exists supremely. Indeed, all and only those things that have a beginning or end, or are made up of parts, as well as whatever does not exist always and everywhere as a whole (as I discussed earlier), can be thought not to exist. The only thing that cannot be thought not to exist is that which has neither beginning nor end, and is not made up of parts, and which no thought discerns except as wholly present always and everywhere.

So you should realize that you can indeed *think* of yourself as not existing even while you know with absolute certainty that you exist. I am amazed that you said you did not know this. For we think of many things as not existing that we know exist, and we think of many things as existing that we know do not exist—not judging, but imagining, that things are as we are thinking of them. And so we can in fact think of something as not existing even while we know that it exists, since we can think the one thing and know the other at the very same time. And yet we cannot think of something as not existing even while we know that it exists, since we cannot think of it as existing and not existing at the same time. So if someone distinguishes the two senses of this statement in this way, he will understand that in one sense nothing can be thought of as not existing when we know that it exists, and in another sense anything besides that than which a greater cannot be thought can be thought not to exist, even when we know that it exists. Thus God alone cannot be thought not to exist, but nonetheless it is also true that there are many things that cannot be thought not to exist while they actually exist. I think, however, that I adequately explained in my book the sense in which God is thought not to exist.[8]

Now as for the other objections you raise against me on behalf of the fool, anyone with much sense at all can easily see through them, so I had judged it best not to bother proving this. But since I hear that some readers think they have some force against me, I will deal with them briefly. First, you repeatedly say that I argue that that which is greater than everything else exists in the understanding; and that if it exists in the understanding, it also exists in reality, for otherwise that which is greater than everything else would not be greater than everything else. Nowhere in anything I said can such an argument be found. For "that which is greater than everything else" and "that than which a greater cannot be thought" do not have the same force in proving that the thing spoken of exists in reality. For if someone says that that than which a greater cannot be thought is not something existing in reality, or is capable of not existing, or can be thought not to exist, he is easily refuted. For whatever does not exist is capable of not existing, and whatever is capable of not existing can be thought not to exist. Now whatever can be thought not to exist, if it does exist, is not that than which a greater cannot be thought. And if it does not exist, it would not be that than which a greater cannot be thought *even if it were to exist*. But it makes no sense to say that that than which a greater cannot be thought, if it exists, is not that than which a greater cannot be thought, and that if it [does not exist but] were to exist, it would not be that than which a greater cannot be thought. It is therefore evident that it exists, that it is not capable of not existing, and that it cannot be thought not to exist. For otherwise, if it exists, it is not the thing spoken of; and if it [does not exist but] were to exist, it would not be the thing spoken of.

This does not seem to be so easily proved with regard to what is said to be greater than everything else. For it is not as evident that something that can be thought not to exist is not that which is greater than everything else that exists, as it is that such a thing is not that than which a greater cannot be thought. Nor is it indubita-

8. See chapter 4 of the *Proslogion*.

ble that if there is something greater than everything else, it is the same as that than which a greater cannot be thought, or that if such a thing were to exist, there would not exist another thing just like it. But these things are certainly true of what is called "that than which a greater cannot be thought." For what if someone were to say that something exists that is greater than everything else that exists, and yet that this very thing can be thought not to exist, and that something greater than it can be thought, although that greater thing does not actually exist? Can it be just as easily inferred in this case that it is not greater than everything else that exists, as it was perfectly certain in the previous case that it was not that than which a greater cannot be thought? In the second case we would need another premise, besides the mere fact that this being is said to be "greater than everything else," whereas in the first case there was no need for anything more than the expression "that than which a greater cannot be thought." Therefore, since "that than which a greater cannot be thought" proves things about itself and through itself that cannot be proved in the same way about what is said to be "greater than everything else," you have unjustly criticized me for saying things I did not say, when they differ greatly from what I actually said.

If, however, this can be proved through some further argument, you should not have criticized me for saying something that can be proved. And that it can in fact be proved should be easily perceived by anyone who knows that it can be proved for that than which a greater cannot be thought. For that than which a greater cannot be thought cannot be understood as anything other than the one thing that is greater than everything else. Therefore, just as that than which a greater cannot be thought is understood and exists in the understanding, and therefore is affirmed to exist in actual fact, even so that which is said to be greater than everything else is with necessity inferred to be understood, to exist in the understanding, and consequently to exist in reality. So you see how right you were to compare me to that stupid man who was willing to affirm the existence of the Lost Island solely because the island would be understood if someone described it.

But you also raise the objection that all sorts of false or doubtful things can be understood, and exist in the understanding, in the very same way as the being I was talking about. I wonder what force you thought this objection could have against me. I was simply trying to prove something that was still in doubt, and for that it was enough for me to show that this being is understood, and exists in the understanding, *in some way or other*, since on that basis the argument would go on to determine whether it exists only in the understanding, like a false thing, or also in reality, like a real thing. For if false and doubtful things are understood, and exist in the understanding, in the sense that one who hears them spoken of understands what the speaker means, there is no reason that the being I was discussing could not be understood or exist in the understanding.

But how can these two claims of yours be consistent: first, that if someone spoke of false things, you would understand whatever he said; and second, that if what you heard is not had in thought in the same way that false things are, you would not say that you think it and have it in your thought, but rather that you understand it and have it in your understanding, since you cannot think this thing without understanding it, that is, comprehending in genuine knowledge that it exists in reality? How, I ask, can these be consistent: that false things are understood, and that to understand is to comprehend in genuine knowledge that something exists? You should realize that this objection has no force against me. If false things can indeed be understood in some sense, and your definition of understanding applies not to all but only to some cases of understanding, then I should not have been criticized for saying that that than which a greater cannot be thought is understood and exists in the understanding even before it was certain that it exists in reality.

Next, you say that it is nearly impossible to believe that when this thing has been spoken of and heard, it cannot be thought not to exist in the way that even God can be thought not to exist. Let those who have acquired even a meager knowledge of disputation and argument reply on my behalf. Is it rational for someone to deny [the existence of] what he understands, simply because it is said to be the same as something [whose existence] he denies because he does not understand it? Or if [its existence] is sometimes denied because it is only partly understood, and it is the same as something that is not understood at all, are not things in doubt more easily proved to be true of what exists in some understanding than of what exists in no understanding? Therefore, it is impossible to believe that someone would deny [the existence of]

that than which a greater cannot be thought, which he understands to some extent when he hears of it, simply because he
denies [the existence of] God, whose meaning he is not thinking
of in any way. Or, if he also denies [the existence of] that than
which a greater cannot be thought, because he does not fully
understand it, is it not easier to prove [the existence of] what is
understood to some extent than to prove what is not understood at
all? So it was not irrational for me to prove against the fool that
God exists by making use of the expression "that than which a
greater cannot be thought," since he would understand that expression to some extent, whereas he might not understand 'God'
at all.

You go to some trouble to show that that than which a greater
cannot be thought is not the same sort of thing as a picture, not yet
painted, in the understanding of the painter, but your argument is
not to the point. I did not bring up the picture that is thought out
beforehand in order to claim that it was the same sort of thing as
the being I was discussing, but merely so I could show that
something exists in the understanding that would not be understood to exist [in reality].

Again, you say that when you hear "that than which a greater
cannot be thought," you cannot think it in accordance with some
thing that you know by genus or species, or have it in your
understanding, since you do not know the thing itself and cannot
infer it on the basis of something similar. But that is clearly wrong.
For since every lesser good, insofar as it is good, is similar to a
greater good, it is clear to every reasonable mind that by raising
our thoughts from lesser goods to greater goods, we can infer a
great deal about that than which a greater cannot be thought on
the basis of those things than which a greater can be thought.
Who, for example, is unable to think (even if he does not believe
that what he thinks exists in reality) that if something that has a
beginning and end is good, then something that has a beginning
but never ceases to exist is much better? And that just as the latter
is better than the former, so something that has neither beginning
nor end is better still, even if it is always moving from the past
through the present into the future? And that something that in
no way needs or is compelled to change or move is far better even
than that, whether any such thing exists in reality or not? Can
such a thing not be thought? Can anything greater than this be

thought? Or rather, is not this an example of inferring that than which a greater cannot be thought on the basis of those things than which a greater can be thought? So there is in fact a way to infer that than which a greater cannot be thought. And so in this way it is easy to refute a fool who does not accept the sacred authority, if he denies that one can infer that than which a greater cannot be thought on the basis of other things. But if an orthodox Christian were to deny this, he should recall that "since the creation of the world the invisible things of God—his everlasting power and divinity—have been clearly seen through the things that have been made" (Romans 1:20).

But even if it were true that that than which a greater cannot be thought cannot be thought or understood, it would not be false that [the expression] "that than which a greater cannot be thought" can be thought and understood. For just as one can use the word 'ineffable', even though the thing that is said to be ineffable cannot be spoken of; and just as 'unthinkable' can be thought, even though the thing to which the word 'unthinkable' applies cannot be thought; in the same way, when someone says "that than which nothing greater can be thought," that which is heard can undoubtedly be thought and understood, even though the thing itself than which a greater cannot be thought cannot be thought or understood.

For even if someone is foolish enough to say that something than which a greater cannot be thought does not exist, he will surely not be shameless enough to say that he cannot understand or think what he is saying. Or, if such a person does turn up, not only should his words be repudiated, but he himself should be ridiculed. So anyone who denies the existence of something than which a greater cannot be thought surely understands and thinks the denial that he is making. Now he cannot understand or think this denial without its parts. And one part of it is "that than which a greater cannot be thought." Therefore, whoever denies this, understands and thinks that than which a greater cannot be thought. Now it is quite clear that something that cannot fail to exist can be thought and understood in the same way. And one who thinks this is thinking something greater than is one who thinks something that can fail to exist. Therefore, if, while he is thinking that than which a greater cannot be thought, he thinks that it can fail to exist, he is not thinking that than which a greater cannot be thought. But it is not possible for the same thing at the same time both to be thought and not to be thought. Therefore, someone who thinks that than which a greater cannot be thought does not think that it can, but rather that it cannot, fail to exist. For this reason the thing that he is thinking exists necessarily, since whatever can fail to exist is not what he is thinking.

I believe I have now shown that my proof in the foregoing book that that than which a greater cannot be thought exists in reality was no weak argument, but a quite conclusive one, one that is not weakened by the force of any objection. For the signification of this expression has such great force that the thing it expresses is, from the mere fact that it is understood or thought, necessarily proved both to exist in reality and to be whatever we ought to believe about the divine nature. Now we believe about the divine nature everything that can be thought, absolutely speaking, better for something to be than not to be. For example, it is better to be eternal than not eternal, good than not good, and indeed goodness itself, rather than not goodness itself. That than which something greater cannot be thought cannot fail to be anything of this sort. So one must believe that that than which a greater cannot be thought is whatever we ought to believe about the divine nature.

I am grateful for your kindness both in your criticisms and in your praise of my book. For since you lavished such great praise on the things you found worthy of acceptance, it is quite clear that you criticized the things that seemed weak to you, not from ill will but in a friendly spirit

GLOSSARY

References to the *Monologion* and *Proslogion* are given by an 'M' or a 'P', respectively, followed by the number of the relevant chapter.

accident: An accident is a feature something has that does not belong to its **essence*** (in sense 2). For example, as Anselm understands it, the essence of a human being is to be rational, animal, and mortal. So any feature that a human being has, other than being rational, animal, and mortal, is an accident. To say that something is "subject to accidents" or "susceptible of accidents" is simply to say that it can have such features that do not belong to its essence.

In M25 Anselm asks whether God is subject to accidents. It would seem that he must be. Such a feature as "being greater than all other natures" seems to be an accident, for example, because it is not part of God's essence to be greater than any other natures. As Anselm argues in M15, if God had not created anything, he would not be the greatest, since there would be nothing else to compare him to. But nothing about his essence would be changed. It therefore seems that being greater than other natures is accidental to God. But if something is subject to accidents, it is changeable, and of course God is supposed to be supremely unchangeable. Anselm's solution to the problem is to distinguish between accidents that do imply a change and those that do not.

body: The word 'body' is used more broadly in philosophy than in ordinary language. Any material object at all is a **body** in the philosophical sense. So chairs and tables are bodies, as are the bodies of human beings and other living creatures.

consubstantial: The Nicene Creed says that God the Son is **consubstantial** with the Father; that is, God the Son is one in being with the Father. Whatever the Father is, the Son is, and vice versa.

It might be helpful for the reader to have the relevant portions of the Nicene Creed. The italicized phrases are those that Anselm deals with explicitly in the *Monologion*. Following each phrase is the number of the chapter in which he argues for that phrase.

I believe in one Lord, Jesus Christ, the only-begotten *Son* (42) of God, begotten of the *Father* (42) *before all worlds* (32), God from God, Light from Light, true God from true God, *begotten* (40–41), *not made* (29), *consubstantial with the Father* (29). *Through him all things were made* (29). . . . I believe in the Holy Spirit, the Lord and Giver of life, *who proceeds from the Father and the Son* (50, 54).

efficient cause: In M6 Anselm distinguishes three sorts of causes. The efficient cause is the one that more or less corresponds to our ordinary English usage of the word 'cause'. The **efficient cause** of x is whatever brings about or produces x. The material cause of a thing is the matter out of which it is made; the instrumental cause of a thing is any tool that was used in bringing it about. To use a standard example, the material cause of a marble statue is the marble it is made of, the instrumental cause is the sculptor's chisel or other tools, and the efficient cause is the sculptor.

In this passage Anselm is generally careful to use different prepositions for each of the three causes. A thing is said to come about "by the agency of" an efficient cause, "from" a material cause, and "by means of" an instrumental cause.

essence: Anselm uses the word '**essence**' in three ways:

(1) It signifies the individual thing that exists. In this usage "an essence" is synonymous with "an existent being."

(2) It signifies the nature of a thing. For example the **essence** of a human being is to be rational, animal, and mortal. Such other features as being tall or short, dark or fair, male or female are **accidents**.*

(3) Occasionally it simply means 'existence'.

essentially: See **substantially/essentially**.

eternal: To say that God is **eternal** is *not* to say that he exists at all times. Rather, it is to say that God exists outside time altogether. That is, he exists in such a way that he has no past, present, or future. All of his existence is simultaneous. Anselm explicates and argues for the doctrine of eternity in M21 and P13 and 18–20.

impassible: This word comes from the Latin '*pati*', "to undergo or suffer," which is contrasted with '*agere*', "to do or act." To say that God is **impassible** therefore means that he cannot suffer or undergo anything. He cannot be acted upon by anything else; he simply acts. Anselm explicates and argues for the doctrine of impassibility in P8.

nature: 'Nature' is interchangeable with **essence*** in both sense (1) and sense (2). When Anselm says that God is a nature, he simply means that God is an individual existent being.

posterior to: There are a number of different ways in which something can be posterior to something else. For example, x is **posterior to** y if (i) x is later in time than y, or (ii) x is caused by y, or (iii) the existence or truth of x is explained by the existence or truth of y, but not vice versa.

quality/quantity/quiddity: These three terms (Anselm uses only the first two) are associated with three different kinds of questions one can ask about a thing. One can ask *"Quid est?"* or "What is it?" The answer to that question will tell you a thing's **quiddity**—in other words, its **essence*** (in sense 2). One can ask *"Qualis est?"* or "What sort of thing is it?" The answer to that question will tell you some **quality** that a thing has, such as justice or goodness. Finally, one can ask *"Quantum est?"* or "How great is it?" The answer to that question will tell you something about the **quantity** of the thing, as for example whether it is great or small. Anselm argues in M16 that when we apply words like 'just' and 'great' to God, they do not signify some quality or quantity of God's. Rather, they signify his essence. For example, justice is not a quality God *has*, as if God were one thing and his justice were some other thing. Rather, justice is what God *is*.

relative: "Daughter," for example, is a **relative** (or "relative term"), since it implies a relation to a parent. Someone is called a daughter, not because of what she is in herself, but because of the relation she has to someone else.

relatively: Anselm claims that **relatives*** are not said **substantially*** of things. In the sentence "Mary is a daughter," 'daughter' is not said substantially of Mary, since it does not signify her essence or substance. Instead, it is said **relatively** of Mary. If instead one said "Mary is rational," 'rational' would be said substantially of Mary, since being rational is part of the essence of being human.

several: The Latin word *'plures'* means "more than one." Wherever possible I have translated it thus; elsewhere I have translated it as 'several'. The reader should therefore keep in mind that 'several' need not imply a large number; it simply implies more than one.

simple: To say that God is **simple** is to say that he has no parts. More specifically, Anselm argues that God has no spatial parts (in M21), no temporal parts (in M21 and P18; see **eternal***), and no metaphysical parts (in M17 and P18).

subsist: 'Subsist' means "to exist (as a substance)." In other words, saying that a substance *subsists* is exactly the same as saying that it *exists*. But **accidents*** do not subsist; they can only exist *in* a substance, not *as* a substance.

subsistent: An individual existent being; a thing that subsists.

substance: The word 'substance' is used in a variety of ways:

(1) It can be used interchangeably with **essence*** in either sense (1) or sense (2).

(2) It can be used to signify the individual thing that underlies **accidents.*** In M79 Anselm argues that individual things are properly called **substances** because they "stand under" (*'substant'*) accidents. Anselm argues in M26 that God can be called a substance in sense (1) but not in sense (2), because he does not, strictly speaking, have any accidents.

(3) It has a technical usage in Trinitarian theology. It was (and remains) customary in the Western Church to speak of God as three persons in one substance, not as three substances. So Anselm realized that his suggestion in M79 that one can speak of God as three substances would be likely to raise eyebrows. He therefore explains in the Prologue that he was following the usage of the Eastern Church, which speaks of the Trinity as being three οὐσίαι in one ὑπόστασις. Since the standard Latin translations for οὐσία and ὑπόστασις are *'substantia'* and *'persona'*, respectively, it turns out that the Eastern Church speaks of God as three substances in one person, and so Anselm's usage is within the scope of orthodoxy.

substantially/essentially: In the sentence "Socrates is human," 'human' is said **substantially** (or **essentially**) of Socrates. That is, 'human' signifies something belonging to Socrates's **substance*** or **essence*** (in sense (2)). Contrast this with 'pale' in "Socrates is pale." Being pale is not part of Socrates's substance or essence, and so in that sentence 'pale' is not said substantially of Socrates. So when Anselm asks what can be said of God substantially, he is asking what terms (if any) signify God's essence. For example, 'Creator' would not be said substantially of God, since it is not part of God's essence to be the Creator. God was, as Anselm would insist, free either to create or not to create, just as he chose. In M15 Anselm argues that certain words are indeed said substantially of God, and he proposes a way of deciding which ones those are.

Sustainer: Recently the practice has arisen of speaking of the Trinity as "Creator, Redeemer, and Sustainer" rather than as "Father, Son, and Holy Spirit." It is therefore important for me to point out that when Anselm uses the word "Sustainer" he is not referring exclusively to the Holy Spirit. When the word is first introduced in M14, it refers to God the Father. Later, after Anselm has argued that all three persons of the Trinity are Creator, we can assume that all three are also Sustainer, since he argues in M13 that the same agency both creates and sustains all things.

unqualified/in an unqualified sense (Latin, *simplex/simpliciter*): According to Anselm, when one says, for example, that a creature is good, one must qualify that statement in various ways. A creature can only be good *in a certain respect* or *for a certain purpose* or *to a certain degree*. God, by contrast, can be called an **unqualified** good, or good **in an unqualified sense**. That is, he is good, period; no qualification of the statement is necessary (or even possible). The same goes for saying that God *exists* in an unqualified sense. Creatures exist *for a time* or *in a certain way* or *to a certain extent*; God just exists, period.

Word: The Prologue to the Gospel according to John states, "In the beginning was the Word. And the Word was with God; and the Word was God. All things were made through him, and without him was nothing made." As Anselm explains it, 'Word' is a particularly apt name for God the Son, since he is God's *utterance* of himself and of creation (see M33). In keeping with these words from Scripture as well as the Nicene Creed (see **consubstantial***), Anselm argues that this utterance or Word existed *in the beginning* (that is, eternally: M32); that he *is God* (M29); and that *all things were made through him* (M29).

INDEX

accidents: 141; as related to immutability, 44–45; God has none, 44–46

Augustine: 3–4, 99 *n.*, 122

belief (*see also* faith): 77, 86–87; in the whole Trinity, 87; necessary for understanding, 99; vs. belief *in*, 88

Boethius: definition of eternity in, 43 *n.*; definition of person in, 88 *n.*

composites: 31–32, 36, 111; all things in time and place are composites, 41, 130–31

craftsman: 15, 122; analogous to God as Creator, 23; disanalogous to God as Creator, 24–25

creatures: changeable, 47; different levels of dignity, 13–14, 50–51, 79–80; do not exist in an unqualified sense, 47–48, 113, 145; exist from God, 15, 18–20; exist through God, 12–15, 18–20; imitate the Word, 50–51, 79–80; made by God, 10, 18–20; made from nothing, 20–22, 113; not nothing before they were made, 22, 55; sustained in existence by God, 26, 47, 113

elements: 18

eternity: definition in Boethius, 43 *n.*; of God: 32–33, 35–44, 47, 107–8, 110–13, 142; of other eternal things, 107–8, 112

existence: in reality vs. in the understanding, 99–100, 121–24, 129, 131–32

existence of God: proof from existence, 12–13; proof from goodness, 10–12; proof from greatness, 12; proof from levels of dignity, 13–15; proofs from "that than which a greater cannot be thought," 99–101

faith: in what is incomprehensible, 77; living vs. dead, 87–88

God: cannot be thought not to exist, 100–101, 125–26, 129–30, 132–34, 136; creatures exist through him, 12–13; does not exist from nothing or through nothing, 15–18; does not *have* but *is* his qualities, 29–31, 107; exists always, 43–44; exists from himself, 15–18; exists everywhere, 42–43; exists in an unqualified sense, 47–48, 113, 145; exists through himself, 12–13, 15–18, 102; good through himself, 10–12, 27; great through himself, 12; greater than can be thought, 109; the Holy Spirit, *see* Spirit; in what sense he is a substance, 45–47, 144; has no accidents (in the strict sense) 44–45, 141; is the